ASSENT TO TRUTH

PETER MORELLO, Ph D

Revised Edition 2015

ISBN 9781500884130

This book is dedicated to Camillo Morello and Rosalia Abate whose love made it possible for me to appreciate the beauty of existence.

Acknowledgements

My gratitude to those who assisted and supported me in this project begins with my mentor while studying in Rome at the Pontifical University of Saint Thomas Aquinas the kindly, late Fr. Richard C. Mathes. Fr. Mathes taught me a vital truth taken from another German Albert the Great the mentor of Aquinas. That truth is that man is not simply a rational animal but a moral animal.

When I decided to write this book I asked Msgr. Charles M. Mangan, himself an author to review it. His response was very positive. Deacon Bob McCormick Administrator and Facilitator of the Permanent Deacon Program Diocese of Rochester, New York reviewed my first draft and offered advice and encouragement.

Also I thank Frank and Mary Capellini who reviewed and edited the initial manuscript and advised on writing for a more general audience. Finally I thank the editors of Create Space for their expertise, patience, and kindness.

Contents

Abbreviations, Texts, and Conventions

Saint Thomas Aquinas:

Sent Ethic *Sententia Libri Ethicorum. Opera Omnia.* Iussu Leonis XIII P.M. Edita. Tomus XLVII. Romae: Ad Sanctae Sabinae, 1969.

Ex Ethic *Ethicorum Aristotelis ad Nicomachum Expositio.* P. Fr. Raymundi M. Spiazzi, O.P. Roma: Marietti, 1949.

Cm Ethic *Commentary on Aristotle*'s *Nicomachean Ethics.* Translated by C.I. Litzinger, O.P. Notre Dame: Dumb Ox Books, 1993.

ST *Summa Theologiae.* Blackfriars. Thomas Gilby, O.P. Leonine and Piana editions. London: Eyre & Spottiswoode, 1963.

Sent De An *Sententia Libri De Anima. Opera Omnia.* Iussu Leonis XIII P.M. Edita. Tomus XLV, 1. Roma: Commissio Leonina, 1984.

CG *Summa contra Gentiles. Opera Omnia.* Iussu Leonis XIII P.M.Liber Tertius. Romae: Typis Riccardi Garroni MCMXXVI.

De Ente *De Ente et Essentia. Opuscula Philosophica.* Raymundi M. Spiazzi. Romae: Marietti, 1954.

Ex Meta *Metaphysicorum Aristotelis Expositio.* M. Cathala, O.P. R. Spiazzi, O.P. Romae: Marietti, 1950.

De Ver *Questiones Disputatae De Veritate. Opera Omnia.* Iussu Leonis XIII. P. M. Edita. Romae: Ad Sanctae Sabinae. 1972.

Virt Cmn *Quaestiones Disputatae De Virtutibus in Communi.* P. Bazzi, M. Calcaterra, T. S. Centi, E. Odetto, and P. M. Pession. Romae: Marietti, 1953.

Virt Card *Quaestiones Disputatae De Virtutibus Cardinalibus.* P. Bazzi, M. Calcaterra, T. S. Centi, E. Odetto, and P. M. Pession. Romae: Marietti, 1953.

Aristotle:

Ethic *Ethicorum Aristotelis ad Nicomachum.* Iussu Leonis XIII P.M. Edita. Tomus XLVII. Romae: Ad Sancta Sabinae, 1969.

The *Sententia Libri Ethicorum, Ethicorum Aristotelis Ad Nicomachum Expositio*, and English Translations of Thomas Aquinas.

The *Sententia Libri Ethicorum* is the result of a commission convened by Pope Leo XIII in the 19th century to edit the works of St. Thomas. It is considered the critical Latin edition of Aquinas' *Commentary* on Aristotle's *Nicomachean Ethics.* Unless noted I will quote C. I. Litzinger's English translation, *Commentary on Aristotle's Nicomachean Ethics*, which at this writing is the sole English translation. Litzinger translated from the *Ethicorum Aristotelis Ad Nicomachum Expositio*, the Cathala-Spiazzi Latin of the Marietti edition. Where there is disparity in translation I will translate the Latin texts of the *Sent Ethic*, as well as others works of Aquinas, into English.

Enumeration of Texts

The enumeration of the Leonine edition *Sent Ethic* are Bekker, whereas the *Ex Ethic* are Cathala-Spiazzi. Consequently the enumeration of texts in the Cathala-Spiazzi Latin texts (*Ex Ethic*) and the Litzinger English translation of Cathala-Spiazzi (*Cm Ethic*) are the same. A major difference is the greater frequency of enumerated sections in the Cathala-Spiazzi. For example, Bekker *Sent Ethic 1143a35-1143b5* is divided into three sections by Cathala-Spiazzi 1247, 1248, and 1249.

Foreword

Deep within each of us there is a desire to know the truth. We want to know what is, what exists, what is real. *Assent to Truth* by the Reverend Peter Morello, Ph.D., offers to the reader a summary of the topics that are closely connected to the search for the truth.

Who may legitimately dispute the importance of sense perception, desire, reason and action, justice, conscience and discernment of spirits in the journey towards knowing? Father Morello is crystal clear: these concepts, along with several others that he confronts, are invaluable for the pilgrimage that is life.

What would take a semester or more in school to draw out Father Morello does in relatively few pages. But let not the length of this vital discussion deceive: these meaty subjects are handled deftly and adequately, and their treatment is a spur to additional reading and study. I, as a believer, was instantly drawn to what the author had to say about Jesus of Nazareth in the search for the truth. I was not disappointed but was roundly inspired—and challenged.

Father Morello has performed a great service. Unhesitatingly, he pushes us to think about what is. In an age known for its vapid and feckless tendencies, the author has identified so much that undergirds our quest for the truth. Father Morello does not let us off the hook. And for that reason, he deserves our thanks. I am inclined to think that even more than our gratitude, he would appreciate our prayers.

Monsignor Charles M. Mangan.

Monsignor Charles M. Mangan of the Diocese of Sioux Falls is author of many essays on the spiritual life. He was appointed to the Vatican's Congregation for Institutes of Consecrated Life and Societies of Apostolic Life by Pope John Paul II.

Preface

King Philip II of Macedonia summoned Aristotle in the year 343 BC to tutor his young son Alexander. Alexander would become the greatest warrior commander the world has known. Sacred Scripture says of him "he advanced to the ends of the earth, plundering nation after nation; the earth grew silent before him, and his ambitious heart swelled with pride" (*1Maccabees 3-4*). What ethical benefit Aristotle's education of Alexander in the virtues and reason had is unclear. What is apparent is that both can be used for self-glorification and evil. Aristotle left the world with a different legacy. He began his search for truth as a biologist studying organic life by meticulous observation. Things had potency, say a caterpillar, to act to be something other. He established that sense perception is the first principal of knowledge and advanced the known sciences including anthropology, ethics, and metaphysics. Aristotle's works were lost through the years but were rediscovered by the Arabs during the 12th century. This was the era of Arabic preeminence in the arts and sciences and the Caliphate of Spain. The famous Arabian Aristotelian scholar philosopher Ibn Rushd was born at Córdoba. Aristotle's works made their way through Spain and Sicily to the Universities of Paris and Naples. Sicily formerly an Emirate formed with Naples the Kingdom of Sicily. Frederick II King of Sicily 1198-1250 and Holy Roman Emperor invited Arab scholars familiar with Aristotle to the royal court at Palermo. He founded the University of Naples where Saint Thomas Aquinas 1265-74 first became acquainted with the genius he would dub The Philosopher.

Aquinas found in Aristotle the most comprehensive thought regarding truth. He continued his academic career at the University of Paris where he advanced Aristotle's rational thought and developed the critical standard of faith and reason.

Social interaction is the common denominator that instills in man, unlike the remainder of animal life an awareness of transcendent truth, of good and evil. The anomaly is this greater awareness of truth often remains obscured. Although our intellect's natural capacity to acknowledge the veracity of things is universal giving assent to the fullness of truth is not. That is a matter of the will. Truth has demands that not everyone wishes to assume. Moral dissipation within modern culture is the primary cause for relativism and the denial of truth. With that denial we subject ourselves to rage, envy, and despair. The pursuit of happiness becomes myth. Sin is the rejection of moral good and the entrée to intellectual error. Philosophy, the pursuit of wisdom has largely transmuted into the pursuit of futile ideas that exist only in the mind. The primary exception is Saint Thomas Aquinas who elucidated timeless premises grounded in existence. He corroborates Aristotle that sense perception is the first principle of all knowledge and accordingly that our actions, not simply our ideas or intent determine what is moral.

If sense perception is the first premise in acquiring truth it needs to be explained what this means and how we proceed. This critical premise then is a first principle, the starting point to further acquisition of knowledge in the arrival at a conclusion. That conclusion is also a principle. This is the process of inference from a singular, the mind's movement from one fact given in experience to another that logically follows. However there are many opinions about the veracity of what is perceived and precisely where to begin as an unimpeachable starting point.

Things change in appearance in accordance with physical variables and even in regard to what we may anticipate. If however we dismiss common sense we will ask what then is certain. And is truth relative? The question of truth remains for many in this age of misleading scientific skepticism unresolved.

The commitment to publish an essay on truth and the responsibility to assent began when a friend, a priest like myself working on a doctorate in Rome asked me the question made infamous by the Roman Procurator of Judea. His thesis, that moral standards are by nature cultural and do not possess permanence was awarded his prestigious university's seal of approval.

So where do we begin? At the start of his treatise on truth *De Veritate* Saint Thomas Aquinas in response to what truth is cites noted Islamic philosopher Ibn Sina that what the intellect first conceives as most evident is being. Knowledge of truth begins with something rudimentary. What we first conceive as most evident, our starting point is the existence of things known through the senses. The unimpeachable premise then is that knowledge of truth begins with sensible perception. As first principle of all knowledge sense perception is the ground to which the order of knowledge and the nature of things correspond. Eternal law is reflected in the order of nature, which doctrine is central to the thought of Aquinas and to the very meaning of truth.

Regrettably the efficacy of sense perception has been cast into doubt and the critical correspondence with reality is broken. This error contributes to misconceptions about the nature of man, reason, justice, conscience, and harmful trends like New Age, Secular Humanism, and Neo Gnosticism. Reality is lost in capricious notions like parallel universes and juxtaposed with virtual reality and illusion.

Rejection of moral good invariably corresponds to intellectual error because the refusal to assent to the former disposes us to refuse assent to intellectual premises that give support to moral truth. Apprehension of truth, which precedes assent, suggests that denial of moral truth is not always due to limited acumen. Fundamental moral wrong such as murder and false witness is evident to all. Conscience and responsibility for good or evil acts resides in this fact. Faith in the apostolic sense is belief confirmed by willingness to carry out the commandments of Christ. Regarding simple belief we must keep in mind that the devils also believed that Jesus is the Messiah, the Holy One of God. Our Christian faith then has its historical origins in the visible witness of the Apostles.

The Eternal Word appeared as man in the world. His words and actions direct human actions. His teaching established that all the virtues are exercised within social interaction, how we treat our fellow man. The truth of our faith then has a rational basis anchored in the physical world and is confirmed by perceivable human actions. The error of the day is that universal ideas of good and the assumed greater benefit they propose outweigh any perceived good of an individual human act. The error of Caiaphas arguing the expediency to condemn to death an innocent man so as to save the nation is repeated.

This study features teaching of the Angelic Doctor inclusive of the contributions of others and demonstrates contrary to modern errors the exclusivity of truth, its universal access, and the superlative value of its possession.

PART I
KNOWLEDGE
1. PERCEPTION

The senses awaken us to reality and our desire to know. We come to love what we experience, what we see and touch. That love, when unfettered from preconceived misunderstanding begins the search for truth and the meaning of life.

Once in the Arizona dusk a white haired Hopi man asked me for a lift. I was pleased to have company on the lonely drive back to Winslow. Night fell quickly. A bright moon rose above the towering Oraibi mesa behind us. I sped across the desert leaving a luminous wake. I hoped to have an interesting conversation.

The Native Americans of our Southwest are a silent, watchful people. They study strangers and do not readily enter into conversation. When he learned I was a priest his gentle face gnarled in anger. "Why did you come here," he demanded, "to convert the Hopi?" The history of the Pueblo people and Catholic Spain took a deadly turn during the Great Pueblo Revolt of 1680 when Franciscan missionaries were hurled off the Mesa I just visited. The Hopi Mesas remain strongholds against external influence. I explained that I had visited his homeland simply out of interest and to enjoy watching the Katchina dances. The Katchina are gods who the Hopi say live atop the San Francisco Peaks that rim the western horizon. They encompass fertility, corn, water, and ancestors. The dances are intended to please the spirit gods. After a period of uneasy silence he said "Father! I am married to a Navajo. She is Catholic. Our daughter was Catholic. My little girl died. Could you tell me where she is?" Surprised by this trust I pondered what to say. I pointed to the sparkling array of stars. "She is there at this very moment smiling down at you."

The elderly Hopi stared at the stars in silence. We reached Winslow. As we parted he grasped my hand and thanked me.

The faint glow of faith was kindled by love for his little girl. The old man envisioned her among the heavenly stars. The Gospels use visible images to convey the immaterial. Christ visibly ascends into the heavens. Heaven is not a place within this universe but is another realm of existence. Analogy is how we understand truths that surpass the visible. Nonetheless discernment begins with sensible perception. We perceive good in things that are good. The smile on an infant's face evokes a sense of purity. Facial expressions should correspond with intent, what is within a person's heart. If not, we are dealing with duplicity. Kindness is perceived in acts. John Steinbeck wrote a short story called *Breakfast* that illustrates this. An invitation by migrant workers to a lone traveler to share breakfast is conveyed solely by expression and gesture.

SKEPTICISM

Skepticism of sense perception of the external world is the basic intellectual error underlying discordance within philosophy, theology, and culture. Descartes applied methodical doubt as the means of isolating an indubitable principal of knowledge. An upright reed appearing bent below water led him to reject the senses. For him indubitable knowledge was knowledge of the self in thought. Hume fueled the skepticism of sense knowledge arguing that perception of things is no more than a bundle of sensations. Knowledge of entities therefore is merely an association of ideas. Likewise the idea of causality is based on repeated events not fact. Experience is reduced to conjecture. Kant says Hume wakened him from slumber. He concluded that in sense perception what we really know is the mind's projection—the so-called phenomenon. The external thing cannot be known in its core reality. The order of knowledge is reversed and truth is thereafter sought within the mind. Truth becomes an arbitrary concept disassociated from reality. By repudiating sense perception these philosophies disclaim the actual order of knowledge and the corresponding order of the nature of things. To the contrary after the fact conjecture cannot misconstrue what is first perceived. Whatever is first given to the intellect as an entity cannot be presumed afterwards to be a collection of sensations.

In sense perception there is a transition from sensing the external object to its cognition by the intellect. Sense perception and cognition by the intellect is one act of knowing (*Sent De An 430a 10-23*). What we know in perception is the thing itself, not the image or phantasm which is actually the conduit through which we know the object perceived. When abstracting knowledge of an object's qualities like color and form, and when we acquire science like refraction of light as in Descartes' bent reed we consciously employ reason and intervals of time. Although subject to reflection sense perception is a quasi reflection (*ST Ia 86, 1 Ad 1*). As such it is immediate and self-evident.

Kant's belief in Hume's 'bundle of sensations' as the initial content of perception, the basis for his doctrine of phenomenon that underpins his philosophical system is imaginary conjecture not given in experience. Kant says the mind has the form prepared to unite the bundle of sensations. That is not possible since the mind must first identify the correct form. It cannot do so based on so-called indiscriminate sensations. The form must therefore be drawn from the perceived object. Noted experimental psychologist Wolfgang Köhler refuted the notion that perception is a bundle of sensations, since "thousands of percepts have characteristics which cannot be derived from the characteristics of their ultimate components, the so-called sensations."[1]

EXISTENTIAL PHENOMENOLOGY

Although philosophy turned inwards in the search for truth there was a renewed focus on existence in the 1900's beginning with phenomenologist Edmund Husserl. He investigated the relation of ideas, or mental phenomena to so-called physical phenomena.

Edith Stein, a Jew turned atheist prior to her conversion to Catholicism 1922 had joined Husserl, also ethnically a Jew, and later Martin Heidegger and Max Scheler in their research and taught philosophy as Husserl's assistant until 1923. Although she received a doctorate *On the Problem of Empathy* from the University of Göttingen 1916 her prerequisite thesis for a chair of philosophy was refused by her mentor Husserl because of her gender and subsequently by the University. Stein espoused women's abilities and thereafter lectured at Catholic affiliated institutions 1923 until prohibited by Nazi Aryan laws in 1933. Formerly a conflicted atheist she now found profound meaning in the Cross. The year Hitler assumed absolute power as Fuehrer of Germany 1934 Stein received the habit of the Discalced Carmelites as Sister Teresa Benedicta of the Cross. She was martyred at Auschwitz [circa 1942], declared a Saint of the Church by John Paul II 1997, and designated daughter of Israel and patroness of Europe.

Husserl propitiously 'bracketed' all assumptions about reality *Ideen* 1913. Professor Timothy Martell says Husserl's 1907 lectures *The Thing and Space* argues perception is the basis for abstract thought and the foundation of our cognitive architecture.

---

[1] Wolfgang Köhler. *Address of the President at the sixty-seventh Annual Convention of the American Psychological Association.* Cincinnati, Ohio, September 6, 1959. American Psychologist. 14 No. 12 (1959) pp. 741-764.

Phenomenologist Max Scheler would say in *The Nature of Sympathy* 1923 it is always some entity that possesses value. Scheler, a Jew who converted to Catholicism and who influenced Edith Stein's philosophy and her conversion fell in conflict with Catholic hierarchy over ethics. Karol Wojtyla future John Paul II wrote his 1953 doctoral thesis on Scheler seeking to reconcile his ethical thought. Wojtyla later published *The Acting Person* based on Scheler and Aquinas in the *Analecta Husserliana* 1969. This nucleus of German mostly ethnically Jewish philosophers is remarkable for their contribution to truth. Martin Heidegger, a non Jew and Nazi Party member 1933 had previously accorded Scheler praise in the search for truth. Heidegger in un-Nazi like terms had said in *Being and Time* 1927 that concern for others demarcates being. Edith Stein's 1918 treatise *Sentient Causality* is compatible to Heidegger's notion of concern. Stein had also resolved Husserl's difficulty in establishing the reality of 'someone else' in her study of empathy. She reasoned sentiments of others are not nominal constituents of perception but adverbial appearances of what is immanent to others. Edith Stein reasons empathy if immanent in me is immanent in others. Compassion is emotive and its perception in another is empathetic. It is a transcendent, metaphysical experience and not a nominal abstraction.[2] Morality is immanent in the person that acts morally.

Edith Stein's approach reflects the phenomenological problem; Kant's premise that we perceive a mental phenomenon and not the real object. Husserl sought to isolate the ground of our perception of reality with the phenomenological reduction which starts with bracketing all assumptions about the perceived object. Stein

---

[2] Edith Stein. *On the Problem of Empathy. The Collected Works of Edith* Stein, Vol. 3, Trans. by Waltraut Stein, PhD. Washington, DC: ICS Publications, 1989. p. 117.

advances the argument for cognition of 'the foreign other' by empathy; that this experience if not primordial is nevertheless manifest to me as primordial. This is common sense fact not conjecture. It sustains discernment and that "empathy is a kind of act of perceiving *sui generis.*" [3]

Edith Stein's contribution to philosophy and ethical awareness is important. It opens the mind to the reality of spiritual discernment, what she terms "religious consciousness," the apprehension of moral states in oneself and in others.[4]

---

[3] Stein, *On the Problem of Empathy.* p. 11.
[4] Stein, *On the Problem of Empathy.* p. 118.

2. DISCERNMENT

BEING

Underlying all that we perceive and commonly understand as reality is the notion of being. Existence is general while being is specific. Aquinas speaks of being in a metaphysical and ultimate sense and in another in relation to human experience. Now man is able to distinguish the reality of his experience from the images that his memory retains. For man that capacity to clearly distinguish external reality from his memory is reflective. That is because in perceiving external things man is also conscious of the self perceiving. He discerns the distinction of his being. Perception then is at once intellectual as well as sensible. And in the wholeness of what is perceived we are thus able to understand the meaning of good.

GOOD

No one can reasonably deny what exists in the same manner that no one can reasonably deny truth. What exists in the mind must correspond to what exists in reality. Being determines what is true in the abstract and what is true independently of ideas. It is not possible to know something without knowledge of what it is. What we discern as good is perceived in things that are good. All being is good. Good then is convertible with being (*ST Ia2ae 18, 3*).

The identification of good with being has to do with God the source of all existence. God is unqualified being and his existence defines the meaning of good. Only God is good in the complete sense. He is unqualified being and perfect good. All things made by God possess goodness to the extent that they fulfill their nature as intended by God. Therefore all created being is good of itself. Man, who God created male and female so as to share an exclusive love one for the other possesses a unique potential for goodness. That goodness extends beyond man's natural capacity. That is due to man's intellect, which mirrors the divinity. Man is reflective in the knowledge of things and as said in knowing them he is conscious of himself. Thus conscious of his being he is able to reflect upon his nature, his purpose for existing, and end. He becomes aware of the supreme truth. By participation in the supreme truth man is deemed good.

FREE WILL

Apprehension for Aquinas encompasses both sensible perception and discernment. Both are an actualization of the intellect and the acquisition of real knowledge. Sensible perception however differs from discernment. Discernment is a deeper understanding of things that involves reflection and reasoning. There is certitude that our discernment is consistent with some general knowledge of reality. For example, the principle free choice is expressed between opposites. That tells us that man is not determined. He has the freedom to move towards either of two opposing ends. Determination is always toward one predictable end. That apprehension is immediate and not proved by reason as if reason were its cause. Rather, it is apprehended through reason. It is the intellect's power to connect a particular discernment to the universal understanding of freedom that gives us certainty. The universal concept freedom does not indicate what it is in acts. It is drawn from acts. Reason infers from this apprehension that man is free and animals determined.

Reason corroborates through observation what is apprehended. Certitude is an interior state of mind that knows truth in the very act of apprehension. And what most separates man from other creatures is the ability to choose between the opposite's moral good and moral evil because of their true polarity and their uniqueness as human knowledge. This framework is intended to facilitate understanding of the more comprehensive treatment of the subject that follows. Moral perception of the correct act is a kind of sense perception; it is initially drawn from physical criteria. Before we act we consider some plan, something we think we ought to do. The envisioned act is the principle of action. Discernment of the act in Aquinas always corresponds to the conditions we sensibly perceive including other, less visible perceived criteria, such as a person's emotional, spiritual state. Deliberation of what the conditions are is followed by our judgment. This judgment is the intellectual apprehension of the morality of the act.

Moral discernment is intuitive due to the act's inherent intelligibility, meaning as a principle of action it is self-evident. But it is not intuition as devoid of reason. Nevertheless the intellect grasps what is true in itself and not what reason makes true. The morality of the act as we shall see below is subject to the scrutiny of the principles of the natural law called *synderesis*. Natural law refers to ends and purpose of things and the way by which man must act in respect to those ends as ordained by God. Aquinas describes the rational link between sense perception and moral action as the exercise of prudence. Prudence remains integral to the apprehension of a moral act in deliberation and in the consequent examination of correspondence to the principles of the natural law.

3. APPREHENSION

Saint Thomas Aquinas' doctrine of apprehension of moral good, i.e. of a good act is drawn from Aristotle's integral doctrines of the order of knowledge and ethics. Aristotle compares the intellect's apprehension of a good act to sense perception in his *Nicomachean Ethics*; "Prudence deals with a singular ultimate, an object not of scientific knowledge but of a kind of sense" (*Ethic 1142a25-30*). He adds "Hence it is necessary that man experience these singulars by sense, and this perception is understanding" (*Ethic 1143b5*.) [5]

Aquinas says that prudence, right reason in deliberating an act approaches its task of knowledge of the correct act, the singular ultimate in step by step reasoning. That discursive process is science. But the intellect apprehends it by simple intuiion (*ST Ia 59, 1 Ad 1*). For Aquinas this intuition is defined as the intellect's final grasp of truth. This apprehension of truth is identified as an inner sense. It is called sense since it is the intellect's judgment of the correct response to what is perceived. Intellectual judgment and sense perception are indelibly linked in moral knowledge

---

[5] Apprehension, the term I use for Aquinas' Latin *intellectus* or intellect is frequently transcribed in English as understanding, intellection, or apprehension. Aristotle and Aquinas use the term intellect when principles are apprehended because only in these instances is the intellect fully actualized. Regarding "a kind of sense" Aristotelian scholar H. Rackham says "The intuition of particular facts which is a part of Prudence also belongs to the genus perception, but it is intellectual, not sensuous" (*Aristotle, Nicomachean Ethics.* London: Harvard University Press, 1994, p. 352).

because the core of moral truth is the act—morality is adverbial and immanent to the acting person.

To illustrate this we begin our assessment of an action with general knowledge of what is good and evil. We understand that murder is evil and that excessive force is evil and why we judge police brutality and indiscriminate killing in warfare reprehensible. And that is why we have trials and inquiries in both cases so as to determine whether a crime was committed. We know from experience that some criminal cases are not clear as to whether they constitute excess or the justifiable use of force. We have a sense of either but when the testimony and evidence for defense and prosecution is presented we may in the end say that it is not a matter of strict science but rather we know it when we see it. Recall Rodney King. Child abuse and pornography often fall under this kind of verdict. Reason helps us get there but it is the intellect that makes the final judgment.

Reasoning must begin somewhere. That is the meaning of principle; it is either the point of departure or the arrival at a conclusion in the reasoning process. As such universal moral principles, our general knowledge of good and evil as well as singular acts are self-evident apprehensions of the intellect. Although Aquinas takes his line of thought on the intuitive nature of knowing principles from Aristotle he finds its corroboration in another source of knowledge, scriptural revelation and the doctrine of angelic creatures. Man may go astray in reasoning toward truth. Angels do not. Angels as well as men nonetheless may go astray in deciding what to do with it. Lucifer is an example. But it is the different ways angels and men arrive at truth that Aquinas is interested in. Angelic creatures are pure intelligence that knows truth directly. Because man's nature is spiritual as well as physical poses whether the end of his discursive reasoning is an act of the intellect that is spiritual by nature and as such transcends the physical.

> For the natural and proper manner of knowing for an angelic nature is to know truth without investigation or movement by reason. But it is proper to human nature to reach the knowledge of truth by investigating and moving from one thing to another (*De Ver 16, 1*).

The intellect in man is potency because we require discursive steps toward the acquisition of knowledge. Man lives in a physical environment and knows through his senses. Reasoning requires images and steps from one point to another in the process of acquiring knowledge. Apprehension here is the knowledge of some truth, a principle acquired at the end of a discursive process. Based on the analogy between the necessity of human discursive reasoning and the direct apprehension of spiritual creatures, apprehension of truth is the intellect's complete actualization. The intellect, except in apprehension, though active is always on the verge of this actualization. Apprehension here is not precisely our normal awareness of this or that as we engage in thinking. Discernment requires willful effort. There is nonetheless an affinity with the angelic intellect in knowing principles. That is due to the spiritual nature of the intellect, since "in so far as it comes in contact with the angelic nature, must both in speculative and practical matters know truth without investigation" (*De Ver 16, 1*).

Acts are either good or evil due to their intelligibility, which is independent of the will or reason. That underscores the importance of apprehension of the singular principle as the concluding judgment of practical reasoning. Insofar as the singular is the object of the practical intellect and the principle of action it holds a certain primacy in respect to the speculative intellect and universal principles of right and wrong.

> Since then prudence is reason concerning an action, the prudent person must have knowledge of both kinds, viz., universals and particulars. But if it is possible for him to have one kind, he ought rather to have the latter, i.e., the knowledge of particulars that are closer to the operation (*Cm Ethic 1194*).

Aquinas means if it were possible to have knowledge of one principle, it is better to have knowledge of the particular, which is the singular principle of action. That is not merely stating a hypothetical. To the contrary he makes it clear in the same text that it is a reality. The following text squarely places priority on the object of practical reason, the act itself.

> But action has to do with singulars. Hence it is that certain people not possessing the knowledge of universals are more effective about some particulars than those who have universal knowledge (*Cm Ethic 1194*).

Synderesis then is that inborn scrutiny of the correspondence of the proposed act to the principles of the natural law. All persons by nature possess general knowledge of the natural law—even if not explicitly. Persons who do not possess explicit knowledge of universals can nevertheless infer the correct act from practical experience.

The singular principle is not the executed act, but rather the correct act as apprehended by the intellect. As such it is a true principle of action "the thing to be done" (*Sent Ethic 1142a23-30*). That is because the choice to execute the action follows its apprehension (*ST Ia2ae 13, 1 Ad 2*). Choice is realized in the external object of the will. That external object is the chosen act. Although reason indicates the correct act anyone is free to choose a different act to suit his or her needs, which may not be morally correct. That is why Aquinas says evil has no formal cause apart from a willed privation of direction to a due end (*ST Ia 49, 1*). An act in which evil is chosen over the apprehended good is always an act that incurs responsibility.

Moral virtue makes reason right. Memory of previous good acts nonetheless plays a role since the correct estimation of principles of action is learned. Example, a physician observes clinical signs and refers to previous modals in his assessment of a patient. But the patient must be clinically assessed before a diagnosis is made.

Knowledge of what is perceived as a good act requires combining and separating. An analogous example is that this animal is a lion. There is previous knowledge strictly in the form of potency of two terms, which are the universal [animal] and singular [lion] (*Sent De An 430a10-17*). Combining and separating in apprehending a thing is the form of understanding what it is (*ST Ia 85, 2 Ad 3*). Aquinas calls this interior act of the intellect the *ratio*. *Ratio* is the judgment that presupposes what a thing is and "what the intellect formulates for itself in order to understand things outside" (*ST Ia 85, 2 Ad 3*). Both in sensible perception of things and in ethical knowledge there is judgment at the moment of apprehension. For ethical apprehension it is the judgment that this act [the singular term] is good [the predicated universal term].

> The intellect is always unerring in knowing first principles; for self-evident principles are those which are immediately known when their terms are understood, because the predicate is part of the definition of the subject (*ST Ia 17, 3 Ad 2*).

The bottom line is that there must first be knowledge of good in the form of potency before the mind draws that knowledge from what it apprehends. The mind cannot identify something unless it somehow already knows what to identify. It is here that Aquinas delineates a middle ground between idealism and realism. But this potency is not actualized knowledge otherwise the mind would be able to draw knowledge of external things from itself. Insofar as moral good is concerned it is the reason why Aquinas says we understand what good is in things that are good. Insofar as the ability to identify that good we already possess a general knowledge of good, the natural law within us in the form of potency. And it is through continuous identification of good in acts that we rationally draw universal principles of that good.

It is upon reflection that the intellect affirms what it apprehends as true or false, gives names to things, and is able to abstract universal objects of knowledge the concepts lion or animal or whole or part and similarly good or evil. Aquinas' mentor Saint Albert the Great correctly added to man's definition moral animal. Man alone can act morally because only man already possesses knowledge in the form of potency to be able to identify and then rationally confirm what is morally good. Acts are first principles that actualize moral good. Again the common understanding of good as universal indicates the nature of an act, not which act.

> The universal is like that which says that such a person must do such a thing: for instance, that a son must honor his parent. Particular reason, however, [says] that this is such and I am such – e.g., that I the son should now display this honor to my parent. The latter opinion produces movement at this time, and not the opinion that is the universal. (*Sent De An 434a16*).

This type of syllogism is akin to what Aquinas calls the operative syllogism. As seen it is apprehension of the singular or proposed act that causes movement [to act] and not the universal. The operative syllogism depicts the intellect's movement from principle to principle on all levels of knowledge, practical and speculative. Logicians are prone to mistake the classic deductive syllogisms that Aquinas makes analogous reference to in the *Sent Ethic* for the operative syllogism, whereas the operative is intended by Aquinas to portray how the mind actually works in apprehending something. The operative syllogism in ethical knowing is the intellect's apprehension of the singular principle of action (*Sent Ethic 1143a35*. This principle is the virtuous mean between excess and defect. It is not a deductive process but a judgment of that action which is apparent to the intellect as a reasonable good.

> Because we acquire knowledge by reasoning, we must proceed from what is better known to us. Now if the better known absolutely is the same as the better known to us, then reason proceeds from principles as in mathematics. If, however, the better known absolutely is different from the better known to us, then we must use the effect-to-cause procedure as in the natural and moral sciences. (*Sent Ethic 1095a30. Cm Ethic 52*).

Good in acts is not necessarily absolute perfection. The cause is the universal moral principle arrived at by inference from the act. The act is the effect. As such it is the remote cause. The statement tells us that in the practice of virtue we arrive at what is *reasonably* understood to be the best option.

Correct measurement isolates a mean between what is known to be excessive and what is known to be defective. If a mean is measured it presupposes knowledge of what is best. The capacity to distinguish excess from defect assumes that. But to arrive close to the mean is sufficient (*ST Ia2ae 66, 1*). We see in the ethics of Aquinas a very reasonable approach to the human condition. Prudence differs from the rigid exactness found in casuistic ethical doctrines that leave little room for deliberation of the conditions that affect the nature of an act. Casuistry has its place but cannot replace the virtue prudence. Example: Aquinas' ethics allows for someone to secretly take—excepting use of force and causing harm from the possessions of another when in dire need. All things created by God are for the benefit of all. The accumulation of goods by individuals should not deprive the community of its needs. Saint Alphonsus Ligouri would later explicate this. We encounter examples of this in recent history when Native Americans in the Amazon rain forests assumed the use of parts of the forests that the government has designated its property.

SINGULAR PRINCIPLE

The teaching of Saint Thomas Aquinas has often been misrepresented. This is especially true regarding the singular principle of action. The reasons are varied. Insofar as his ethical doctrine is concerned a comprehensive study was never made partly because Aquinas' ethics is not compiled in one work but is distributed throughout his works. Due to the absence of a comprehensive study and conflicting views numbers of Catholic professors have turned to fixed systems like Kantian ethics, a system that ultimately depends on the authority of dictum rather than moral judgment. It is abundantly clear that the doctrine of a singular principle of action is an indispensable truth and the cornerstone of sound ethical doctrine. Apprehension of the singular then is not due to necessary inference from the universal. That would reduce moral discernment to logical deduction. The universal in that instance would be its own cause (*ST Ia 19, 5*). Although logical formulae have a definite place in ethics as guidelines some logicians make the mistake of confusing virtuous behavior with pursuing intricately detailed logical propositions. As Aquinas made clear knowledge of the universal good does not of itself include the moral virtue necessary to acknowledge the singular, which is the correct action and the willingness to do it. Moral virtue has to play the significant role in movement from the universal to performing the act. We apprehend goodness in acts that communicate goodness. Moral virtue enables us to acknowledge the good in things, and to envision compassion and love in what we do.

We are motivated to act by our desires. The will itself is understood as rational desire. Human desires can be purely intellectual as in the desire for power or sensual as in the desire for sexual pleasure. Needless to say with rational man the intellect has the role of directing the will rightly. Rather than being subject to instinct as we find in non rational animals man has the freedom to choose whether and how to respond to desire. In fact that capacity to choose between good acts and evil acts defines ethics and what it means to be human. I will continue to repeat this vital truth that what most separates man from the remainder of the animal kingdom is not simply his level of intelligence. It is rather the capacity to distinguish and select between opposites and most specifically the opposites good and evil in a human act. Any creature can select from a menu. That ability is not the expression of free choice in selecting an opposite. Animals are determined by nature to specific ends and if hungry will eat. Man has the freedom to choose the manner by which he responds to his desires. He can choose a moral good and even if hungry may not eat what is his and select an opposite, which is to offer his food to another in greater need. The issue is those desires that are part of human nature and which present moral options and those that deviate from human nature and lead to immoral acts.

Man possesses the capacity to make the distinction between good and evil through his intellect. Now the human intellect cannot be compared analogously to animal intelligence because with man we are not dealing with what is often thought simply a higher degree of intelligence. Reflective of himself, of his distinct person in the act of perceiving something man reasons and contemplates the meaning of things. Man exhibits intellectual features that transcend the physical. When perceiving he has the ability to apprehend a spiritual dimension to his being. He considers the meaning of his life questioning whether he is immortal, is there life after death. Man is naturally conscious of values pertaining to his person and is able as pointed out by Edith Stein to acknowledge similar innate goods belonging to other persons. The ancient dictum do onto others is the fundamental natural law premise that all men possess. Man apprehends truths that define human nature and individual rights. He then more deeply comprehends their meaning and application through discernment. Finally he deliberates the correct manner in applying this knowledge to his actions.

PART II
REASON
1. DESIRE

Desires are naturally inclined to what gives pleasure, and most important happiness. They delineate man's nature. All of us understand what we are by that which fulfills us. That understanding is clearly evident in the relationship between a man and woman. Man was created in God's image, male and female He created them. A man by nature loves the pleasure and company of a woman. That is evident when he seeks to engage in a lasting relationship. He knows that she provides something that is lacking in him. She by nature shares the same attraction. They perceive in their specificity as male and female that which defines man as a unity bonded in mutual care, as providers, nurturers, and protectors of children that are the evidence of love for each other. That bringing into the world of new life to be cherished and taught what is true makes them co-creators. It cultivates in them an understanding of the spiritual beauty of life that speaks to their hearts of the goodness of the Divine Creator.

What man is and his ultimate end are ordained by God. Unlike animals which are inclined by instinct reason sets man apart. The word desire encompasses two meanings distinguished by Aquinas. The first is appetite and the second inclination. Appetite [often translated as desire] refers to an initial attraction stimulated by some external good (*ST Ia 59, 1*). Appetites initiate the inclinations, which remain natural and good to the extent that they are reasoned and adhere to the laws of nature. This is Aquinas' rationale for separating appetite from inclination. It clarifies not simply behavior but what is moral. Inclinations can be attributed to the mind, to the will, and to sensible desires, the latter called passions. Desires that are in us by nature always aim at what is ordained as good. For example the initial movement of the sensitive appetitive faculties [let us say smell] is due to the impression upon it of the external agency of some good [a barbecue]. The reasoned appetites form those inclinations that supersede man's sensitive appetites. So if not invited to your neighbor's barbecue reason informs us not to take it. Reason thereby inclines both the rational appetite, the will, and the sensitive appetites or passions such as love, anger, desire. From here on in the term desire will be used as inclusive of but distinguished when needed of the appetites and inclinations described by Aquinas. Aquinas adds that reason motivated by moral virtue makes our initial desires right in their tendency toward acts. The process includes the transposition in man of the forms of what is sensibly desired to the intellectual desires. The intellect is able to distinguish the moral good inherent in things (*Sent Ethic 1139a27*). The intellectual desires include activity related to autonomous motivation combined with comprehension and belong to the rational part of man. Intellectual desires also differ from sense desires because of the object desired by the intellect. Such are the desire for knowledge, academic accomplishment, and the desire to know and love God. The desire for power oft deemed detrimental is intellectual. The will then is intellectual desire (*ST Ia 19, 5*). To will is to decide; it is an act of the intellect. A correct inclination is desire directed by the will to its proper end. The rational dimension of man is consequently twofold. The first is the intellect which is rational by nature and the other is the desires, which are rational by participation, thus forming our inclinations.

Specifying what something is not can clarify what it is. Behavior scientists provide this opportunity. Important contributions to understanding human behavior have been made. Among the more prominent Carl Jung's agnosticism and Sigmund Freud's atheism are typical of scientists that generally consider religion a hindrance to mental health. That so they are not disposed to a comprehensive understanding of man. The result is polarization between much of mental health science and traditional ethics generated by the former's repudiation of an inherent spiritual aptitude toward moral good. Psychologists and psychoanalysts tend to view their science as definitive and apart from direction toward basic needs do not recognize a natural law in man. The public tends to believe that if suppositions are called scientific they must be true. The presumption that all behaviors have no other natural propensity than to achieve expedient ends in relation to food, sexuality, survival, acceptance, and security has encouraged the move toward an amoral secular culture. Lacking the right starting point for studying desires they borrow hypotheses from sciences not directly related to the study of human behavior.

Naturalist Charles Darwin held that animal nature is determined by the necessity of species to adapt. This precipitates the process of natural selection. The strongest and more intelligent survive to improve and continue the species. Sociologist Herbert Spencer began the trend of comparative analysis between animal and human behavior when he applied natural selection to social and economic theory. His presumption was that all animal behavior is essentially the same and therefore the principle of natural selection must apply to human behavior. The brightest and the strongest are destined to be successful while the poor inherently lack those qualities. Today with the popularity of equanimity in socio-economic matters that bias is contested, but not entirely abandoned by some. David Barash professor of psychology at the University of Washington who like Spencer applies Darwin's evolutionary principles of animals to the psychology of human behavior. Barash argues in *The Myth of Monogamy: Fidelity and Infidelity in Animals and People* that traditional sexual ethics are artificial. B.J. Skinner's doctrine of behaviorism addresses the plausible need for human adaptation to environment and the option of natural selection. But behavioral traits and character are in effect entirely determined in response to environment. Mathematician Ivan Pavlov influenced Skinner and others in his numerical study of animal behavior in response to stimuli and repetitive reinforcement to response.

Notwithstanding the trend toward the comparison of human behavior to non-rational animal behavior others have raised the bar of what it means to be human. Psychologist Carl Rogers' theory of orgasmic valuing is about the instinct to sense physical good or bad. This inner ability to sensibly discriminate moves to the next level of the need for love, attention, nurturing. At this level however Rogers presents us with a humanistic theory of societal positive and negative reinforcement that shapes our self-esteem. Beyond that there is little said about the reasoned discrimination of good or evil behavior. Rogers does acknowledge a natural law in man, insofar as it is limited to the level of non-rational creatures. That view includes Abraham Maslow and his hierarchy of needs, which begins with the animal need for food, water, and sex and the more rational needs for safety, and belonging and love. The rational inclination of desires is viewed by most psychologists in the context of mental health and personal actualization. While there are recognized similarities between human and animal behavior what is largely missing in psychology is a doctrine of moral virtue that completes the definition of man.

Trait is a psychological term that in some respects, depending on usage compares with appetite but is often more in line with inclinations that are elective. As seen, there are in man inclinations that belong to human nature. But while learning is a factor some psychologists hold that all human inclinations are strictly the product of learned behavior. Others differ. Clinical and often experimental psychologists study persons directly rather than hypothetically and come closer to recognition of a natural law inherent in man. Karen Horney and Erik Erikson have observed unlearned behavior patterns or so-called traits that are particular to male children and traits that are particular to female children. Psychiatrist Karl Stern, former President of the Canadian Psychiatric Association notes in his work *The Flight from Woman* a biological law of human sexuality, of native feminine and masculine inclinations that is the underlying structure for mental health. Interestingly Sigmund Freud made similar observations. His early training in neurology was related to his ambition to discover the bedrock of psychology. Bedrock was the term used by Freud in *Analysis Terminable and Interminable* as the final strata that underlie the differences that distinguish male and female sexual inclinations and behavior patterns. His remarkable conclusion was "for the psychical field, the biological field does in fact play the part of the underlying bedrock". [6]

Karl Stern and Sigmund Freud perceived a sexual duality in men, the male dynamic being the dominant of the two. Freud does not equate passivity in males with effeminacy, although in therapeutic counsel he perceived in support of what Stern would

---

[6] Sigmund Freud. *Analysis Terminable and Interminable.* (*1937*), *vol. 23.* The Standard Edition of the Complete Works of Sigmund Freud. Ed. and trans. by James Strachey. London: Hogarth Press, 1971. p. 253.

observe, an obstinate resistance in men to passivity. He again attributed that resistance to biological bedrock, not physical difference. Stern and Freud are in agreement that the feminine passive [as distinguished from adapted effeminate behavior in men that mimics women] are an integral and vital component of healthy male psychology.

Ancient cultures acknowledged differences in masculine and feminine. If a male exhibited behavior that identified with the feminine, it was usually considered extraneous to normal behavior. Greek literature, art and poetry indicate homosexuality was tolerated. However homosexual practice is typically viewed by most cultures to diverge from the more widely accepted pattern of male and female behavior. There is no evidence of same sex marriage in human history. Aquinas' position on homosexuality was elicited from historical accounts, animal behavior, and the teachings of the Church the latter invariably confirming *Rm 1: 1*. There were exceptions but they remain for the Church deviations from the divinely instituted natural order.

> Some wrongdoing is specially called unnatural because it goes against even animal nature: homosexual acts, for example, which run counter to the natural mode of intercourse between male and female (*ST Ia2ae 94, 3 Ad 2*).

Aside from biological and emotional particularity in male female behavior there is deeply rooted spiritual difference. From Saint Thomas Aquinas' metaphysical standpoint the form is the act of the soul upon matter that specifies what something is. Biology is the spiritual stamp on the physical. Behavior, because of free will, can be altered. Significantly it is the Creator who provides the very act of existence. This adds a spiritual dimension that underlies what a being is in the specificity of the form, which for man is immortal. For example after death and prior to the resurrection of the body the soul of a person remains what it was originally intended by the Creator. Men remain men and women remain women inclusive of their particularities, feminine and masculine. Given the biological, emotional, and spiritual differences between male and female, and especially the fact that those differences compliment their relationship and the continuance of the human race it is unreasonable to assume that exceptions, or even a growing proclivity in modern culture make a natural rule. The Author of Life ordained sexual love to be nothing other than between a man and a woman. Unfortunately man is capable of deviation from what is inherently natural to his person. Deviate behavior can be learned and proliferated. There are instances that seem otherwise in some persons from childhood. Aquinas recognized rare intrinsic aberrations in the natural law citing that "natures subject to generation and corruption fail in some few cases on account of some obstacle" (*ST Ia2ae 94*, *4*). There are known cases of natal deformities that include hormonal deficit. Research at Berkeley suggesting similar effects by environmental toxins have to date not provided evidence. Ultimately compassion should be the rule.

Aquinas' doctrine of an unchanging natural law can be accommodated in a pluralistic society despite opposition from those who assume the false premise that male and female has no more than physiological significance. What Aquinas had in Christianity, notwithstanding the influence of Aristotle, is a far more cohesive perspective of what it means to be a man or a woman. In the Christian milieu we have acceptable forms of passivity, gentleness and humility that are considered necessary for the smooth functioning of society. That needless to say was especially true for the friar living in community. But Christians and Jews also have extraordinary female role models. The recent beatification of Joan of Arc, to whom Saint Therese of Lisieux was devoted recognizes another if rare capacity. Deborah became judge and military protector of the Jewish people. The beautiful Judith used the ploy of seduction to behead the Jew's enemy Holofernes. She later became their judge. All and particularly priests should look to the Blessed Virgin as an exemplar of both humility and fortitude. The notably manly John Paul II emulated Christ's love for His Mother, and her virtues. The remarkable world wide appeal of his spirituality and courage can be attributed to that devotion. The Christian sexual modal seen in the lives of the saints is one of reasonableness, the respect of life, advancement of family, gracious culture, courage, and spiritual beauty.

Homosexuality and gay marriage is held by many Christians, Jews, and Muslims to be elective and accidental to the will in respect to sin, in other words sinful. Others hold that such behavior is indicative of changes in nature itself. Another perspective favored by gay life style advocates is that sexual behavior is elective by right because laws of nature do not exist. Life is said to be open to reasoned variations and are not contradictory. The fallacy of that position is that if there is no intrinsic direction of male female sexual behavior then history contradicts itself. Fallacies which hold that human nature is changing or that there are no natural laws governing sexuality if universally accepted—as they seem on the verge of—will result in the disintegration of family structure and the ruin of human life. Disordered sexual relationships are not father and mother familial structures. We do not find that kind of increase in other animal species. The indications are that male and female sexual orientation is determined by nature and that same sex behavior is typically elective. However psycho-social orientation influences sexual behavior and may lessen free choice and moral responsibility.

Men and women share equal status insofar as their necessary complementary roles. Unfortunately in every age men are presumed superior to women because of greater physical strength, physical courage, and leadership ability. Women nonetheless possess these virtues but exhibit them differently. Women tend to be more person oriented than men are and often exhibit important dynamics that men overlook. That of itself is leadership in showing men ways to avoid conflict. Women have demonstrated extraordinary leadership ability beyond the ordinary.

Aquinas isolates inclinations that are not initially driven by nature. The latter are behavior patterns that are acquired and particular to this or that person.

> For many of them are not immediately prompted by nature, but have to be investigated and are reasoned out before they are held to be helpful to the good life (*ST Ia2ae 94, 3 Ad 1*).

That investigation is a function of ethics. In review the rational dimension of man then is twofold. The first is the intellect, which is rational by nature; the other is sensual desire, which is rational by participation. Intellectual desires in man include the free motivation of the will, which is the choice whether to pursue the object of desire, and the manner in which that object is pursued. These intellectual inclinations are myriad and constitute a personality. They include *synderesis* and others affected by memory of effect that variously incline us and are the basis for conscience. Rational desire is the will (*ST Ia 19, 5*) which acts in unison with the intellect (*ST Ia2ae 13, 1*). Accordingly reasoned inclination of desire and virtuous action is the object of prudence. Desire if natural is always toward some good. There is nevertheless the possibility of deviation either in abhorrence and avoidance or in the impulsive, uninhibited pursuit of pleasure. Desire in this instance is acquired and unnatural (*ST Ia2ae 30, 3*). Other elective inclinations are adapted to meet physical health needs and most important the cultivation of moral habits, such as are helpful to the good life mentioned above.

Aquinas in *ST Ia2ae 30, 1* also speaks simply of the irrational and natural desire toward some sensual good. He makes no mention of sin in the desire. In contrast he distinguishes "Lust" in *ST 2a2ae 153, 1* as that *rational* desire which belongs to some illicit venereal pleasure, thereby distinguishing lust as a willful movement toward evil. Aquinas' position delineates the proper sequential process of discernment that begins with apprehension in the form of sensible knowledge, followed by desire, and the judgment of reason. It confirms that there are initial, natural sexual inclinations that are neither the effect of sin nor the result of sin.

The key to mental health is a candid awareness of all our human desires. Insofar as a man's natural desire for a woman is not genital but aesthetic it is good. And if there is transient desire for such sexual contact it is not a deadly sin if it is resisted. That is the meaning of resisting temptation. Lust requires consent. If we know it is wrong it indicates a tendency that was not originally intrinsic to man [God did not create man to be evil], but is instead the legacy of original sin.

Attraction for the opposite sex is intrinsic to human nature. Repression of natural desire, to try to obliterate it as if the attraction itself is sinful is a disordered judgment that may precipitate further disorder in the form of sexual expression. Sexual attraction is natural whereas sensuality, the indiscriminate inclination for sensual gratification is not. Sensuality akin to lust is deadly. A disordered will predisposes us to inordinate attraction. That is why when someone of the opposite sex appears we often fail to consider them daughter or son, mother or father and so forth. Without grace and awareness of the intrinsic good it reveals in persons we tend to look on their physical beauty as reason for self gratification, a violation of their person. Grace transforms our perception and tempers attraction. It rectifies the inclinations. Perfect temperance then is motivated by spiritual love of neighbor. Union with God encourages withdrawal from sensual gratification and a more selfless love of neighbor.

Author and ethicist Martha Nussbaum embraces the Epicurean view that religion is *belief-disease* and an intellectual illness that inhibits therapeutic activity. She adds Thomas Aquinas' *Summa Theologiae* is an example of such a widely disseminated belief disease wrongly drawn from Aristotle's ethics.[7] Her position is the stereotyped version of religious philosophy that suppresses healthy thought and life styles for sake of the ulterior motive of salvation. She places the concept of soul as an abject version of the mind and its real therapeutic needs. Her knowledge of Greek philosophy however constrained due to an apparent agnosticism plus her knowledge of psychology provide a good backdrop for better understanding of the issues we face regarding religious belief and modern science, in particular ethics.

Now Hellenistic ethical philosophy invariably includes awareness of the overall good of others, such as avoiding the infliction of injury, and personal well being. Nussbaum concedes that Aristotle's dialectic commitment to moral values as compared to Epicurus' narrow focus on the preeminence of the individual has a place in the overall medical ethical analogy. Aristotelian values

---

[7] Martha C. Nussbaum. *The Therapy of Desire.* Princeton, NJ: Princeton University Press, 1994. p. 137.

are deemed by her to mean procedural virtues that encompass the "dialectical scrutiny of opposing positions, mutual critical activity, and perspicuous ordering." However Aristotle's *Ethic* contains unalterable moral principles which Nussbaum omits, which has been summarized in a *Thomist* article.[8] Aquinas does not make that omission in his commentary on Aristotle in the *Sent Ethic* or elsewhere. Adultery and murder, for example, are inherently evil acts, and in order for them to be morally good they must be subject to a virtuous mean between excess and defect (*Sent Ethic 1107a22-27*). That is impossible according to Aristotle as well as Aquinas.

Nussbaum does not repudiate the existence of God. Rather, she finds fault in what she sees as conventional religion's inflexible mores. What she does not recognize is that goodness in acts is behavior that finds its ultimate source in the supreme good. But if the ethicist convinces herself there is no supreme good she may not be disposed to identify acts that are absolutely good or evil, even when set plainly before her by Aristotle. For Aristotle and Aquinas the ultimate end is always found in the means to the end. The coherence between ends of acts and right reasoning in pursuit of the higher good define the ethics of both philosophers.

Happiness is the ultimate end of the eudaemonist ethics of Aristotle. He considers contemplation of truth the ultimate source of happiness. It is more evident in Aquinas, though not precluded by Aristotle that the supreme good is found in God. Notwithstanding her omission Nussbaum recognizes that mutual discourse ethics risks reduction to the client's self gratification if focused on Epicurean individualism. And ethical good cannot be identified if limited to mere procedural values. Nussbaum

---

[8] Christopher Kaczor, *Exceptionless Norms in Aristotle?: Thomas Aquinas and Twentieth Century Interpreters of the Nicomachean Ethics,* The Thomist. 61 (1997). p. 43.

however finds in Epicureanism a therapeutic value superior to Aristotle's procedural values. She discovers in this approach the honesty needed to recognize what she alludes to as unconscious layers of motivation that may free the client from society's obsession with wealth and status. But effective appraisal of needs and desires depends on some sense of good that counters self-indulgence. Reason if impartial is always ordered to that good. A person however irreligious may possess that sense. Hellenistic philosophy's commitment to logic and empathy coupled with Stoic detachment is arguably attractive. That is especially true for an author who is suspicious of formal religion. She is nonetheless correct to the extent that if we wish to uncover bedrock in human nature it is quite reasonable to begin with what is fundamental to it, desires.

Nussbaum, despite her suspicions, makes a very important observation. She says that the revulsion to religious love of god is often followed by an idolatry of the person loved that results in violence. Whether there is need to love passionately and how to fittingly do so is not adequately treated by her except for her observation that Hellenistic freedom from disturbance seems dispassionate and aloof. Nussbaum sees the difficulties of expressing passion and anger and of vulnerability in human love. Summarizing she recommends abandoning religion and "the zeal for absolute perfection," and extols empathy for "the ambivalent excellence and passion of a human life."[9] The former is not the problem in Aquinas and the latter "ambivalent excellence" is gloss. The problem is Stoic and Epicurean lack of a proper object for unreserved passion. Persons can only be loved in the measure that is appropriate to their limited nature. Emotions find balance in unreserved love of God, the supreme good that motivates us to act

---

[9] Nussbaum. *The Therapy of Desire.* pp. 507-10.

with compassion. But to her credit Nussbaum discerns the stabilizing effect of love for God in the passionate love for another person. Nussbaum also recognizes that that which is best is a moderate good disclosed by reason. A moderate good nonetheless is the virtuous mean between excess and defect. Nussbaum would agree that there are reasonably discerned excessive as well as defective behaviors. Nevertheless the mean of virtue reduced to personal need does not indicate free choice. Animals do the same.

A feeling of want is right when reason inclines it. If excess or defect have meaning at all and are to be avoided the mind and not passion makes that determination. The pursuit of good admits to actions that are by nature unjust. This does not deny that Martha Nussbaum makes good ethical decisions even if she rejects immutable moral principles in her book. It simply means that there is a more coherent way of describing ethics and being more consistent in arriving at good conclusions. Martha Nussbaum fails to recognize that immutable principles do not restrict flexibility. Assessment of the conditions of an action may show that other principles apply than those first thought to. The fear that freedom is betrayed if we admit to fixed norms is baseless. Unalterable principles possess the expansiveness that can only extend freedom of action because acts are not narrowly consigned to personal interests.

The salient point of *The Therapy of Desire* is that it correctly centers ethics on human desires and passion and speaks to, or least should to a reasonable mean. Certainly if we were to ground ethics in anthropology this is where to start. That is where Aristotle begins his *Ethic.* The ends of acts are first perceived as ends of nature. Those ends are apprehended in our initial desires for something appealing, something that gives pleasure and satisfaction. It follows that ethics begins with the rational inclination of desires (*Sent Ethic 1103a3*). Right reason is focused on the means to the end and not the end understood as desire alone. Right reason is the freedom to think without a priori restrictions as to what is best. Whether belief in a supreme good is therapeutic or not should be the consideration for ethicists rather than outright rejection because of suspicion of religion. Why should not the greatest good be considered if that belief is shown to produce detached and compassionate behavior? Detachment in this instance is not apathy and dispassion because its focus is on an external good that has internal therapeutic value. It is not self-serving. People are lifted out of despair. The disparaging belief that life is an apathetic quest for self-satisfaction minimizes our zest for life as well as our humanness. Moral reasoning is limited when the focus of attention is given to expediency in avoiding excessive passion and affiliated affliction. That would reduce ethics to the avoidance of physical and emotional evil perceived by the individual.

Passion is evident in both human love and in divine love. It would seem that human love is rendered innocuous if passionate desire were eliminated. The recognition that excess and defect impinges on a spiritual balance that is measured by love of God is all-important. Within a life centered on love of God human passions are tempered by adherence to a way of life. It is a life of mutual respect and the nurturing of another's unique person and talents. Passionate love for another human as is appropriate only between man and woman is fully realized as a self giving commitment to the good of that person. Sexual desire has within it the natural element of passion. When coupled with love of God that love does not degrade to idolatry and inevitable destructive behavior. To have a passionate desire for God has equivalence in loving others as Christ has loved us.

Nussbaum's study of desire suggests that God is the correct end for that powerful human sentiment called passion. Passion, the ultimate expression of desire is not adequately addressed in classical Greek ethics or in Nussbaum's study because the counterbalance of the supreme good and the natural reasoned tendency to that supreme good is omitted by the former and not fully explored by the latter. Nussbaum's insight that belief in God tempers passion to a rational level of behavior should be addressed by her in the future. It admits to a dimension of desire that belongs specifically to human nature. We see it throughout history. If it is not appropriate when fully directed toward other humans the indication is that there is a correct end, which is God.

Catherine of Siena conveys Our Lord's counsel on passion for purification of the Church.

> I promise you, that, by this means her beauty will be restored to her, not by knife or by cruelty, but peacefully, by humble and continued prayer, by sweat and the tears shed by the fiery desire of My servants, and thus I will fulfill your desire if you, on your part, endure much, casting the light of your patience into the darkness.[10]

---

[10]Catherine of Siena. *The Dialogue of the Seraphic Virgin Catherine of Siena, no. 34.* Edited by Algar Thorold. London: Kegan Paul, Trench, Trubner & Co., Ltd. 1907.

2. PRUDENCE

Right reason in the deliberation of acts defines the virtue prudence. It is the natural capacity to assess our actions and act morally. It is not simply the envisioned beneficial or detrimental effect of our actions, but whether the act is itself good or evil.

The good of what we think and what we say is always confirmed by what we do. Intent as well as the choice of act, and its object [what it does] must be good. The circumstances must be good. Virtue in ethics is ultimately situated in human acts. Now while all of us reason practically in what we do there is a right way of reasoning that leads to the choice of good acts. Right reason in acts complies with the order of nature and revealed truth. Reason perfects the virtues that are natural to man. Prudence then is also a natural, intellectual virtue. For example, a man can deliberate the right way of guiding a ship and consequently act rightly. Virtue, to be moral virtue requires prudence on a higher level of perfection than the ability to correctly guide a ship or manage an office. The latter is simple or natural prudence (*ST 2a2ae 47, 2*). Man acquires moral virtue through right reasoning on the good or evil of acts. Moral virtue is in the choice of good acts as opposed to those that are evil—regardless of whether a desired good effect is achieved. Again, it is not the good effect alone that makes an act good.

Prudence simply defined is reason concerning an action. Ethics is always concerned with good acts. To better comprehend what it means for an act to be good we can look at it in the context of its effects. Some make the mistaken argument that in cases when an act has both a good effect and an evil effect, commonly called a double effect the greater proportion of the good effect admits to condoning an evil act. Whereas the effect of an act does not make an act good or evil understandably all acts should have a good effect. We are likely familiar with well intended and well chosen acts that inadvertently go awry. While the act may result in some unexpected physical evil the act is not morally evil. Aquinas treats the issue of an act with two such effects in *ST 2a2ae 64, 7* in respect to self defense and the death of an assailant. The accepted premise is that all persons have the right to defend themselves from physical attack. The act is morally evil if in self-defense one chooses excessive force. Otherwise the act although resulting in a physical evil is permissible. The application of the principle today is largely in medical care where we are dealing with physical effects. An example is the correct proportion in removing an infected leg to save a life. However whenever the principle of double effect is mistakenly applied to an act such as abortion we are not simply treating a proportionate good or evil physical effect but an act that is the deliberate taking of an innocent life. It is therefore intrinsically evil. The evil of the act censures any argument based on a proportionate good effect. The principle does measure up to a good medical decision when death is unintended and every measure is taken to save life. An example is a caesarean procedure intended to save mother and infant and death occurs.

Aquinas acknowledged Aristotle's observation that man may acquire moral virtue through reason, and that prudence on this natural level of acquisition is called perfect prudence (*Sent Ethic 1144b1*). Moral virtue however, including the virtue prudence does not find its perfection through reason alone as thought by Aristotle. We find in Saint Thomas Aquinas the added distinction of prudence perfected both by reason and the infused virtues that are the gifts of the Holy Spirit. He separates moral virtue naturally acquired through reason from that moral virtue which includes reason and is the effect of grace necessary for salvation. Virtuous behavior necessary for man's salvation has a specified end. Aristotle said in his *Ethic* that the ultimate end of virtue is happiness, a perfect good (*Ethic 1097b6-16*). He says God is the principal cause of happiness (*Ethic 1099b14-18*). Aquinas' commentary on Aristotle's *Ethic* adds that man must also have knowledge of his ultimate end, which is God. Knowledge of God must include knowledge of a higher spiritual ordering of our actions.

> All humanity must be ordered to the supreme and ultimate end of human life. It is therefore necessary that man have knowledge of his ultimate end. The reason is this that the ultimate end is always found in the means to the end, which must also be ordained to the ultimate end itself (*Sent Ethic 1094a22-24.* Translation is mine).

The supreme good of a human act is its being ordered to man's ultimate end in God. Furthermore the supreme good can never be removed from the means to the end of acts. Ethics would otherwise find its measure in intended advantageous outcomes, conceptual hypotheses that are given reality by the mind rather than in an objective good found in the concrete intelligibility of the good of the act. That is because good and evil are eminently manifest in acts and not thought. The end of virtue is a virtuous act.

As said the mean of an act refers to the delineation between excess and defect. Using the example of double effect it can be understood as the use of excessive force in self-defense as opposed to the defect of posing no resistance, let us say if a parent makes no effort to protect their child from abuse. The virtuous mean, which is neither excessive nor defective, is the *proximate end*, the envisioned choice of the act resulting from deliberation. Virtue is the congruence of intent and choice of act. It defines the act's object, which is what the act itself is about. For example is it designed to kill or protect. Moral virtue is what makes the person pursue the good for its own sake. The supreme good becomes the object of the will as it is judged by reason. This is primarily why Aquinas' ethics is called virtue ethics.[11] That is because it requires moral virtue to pursue what is best.

Although reason determines virtue in acts there is also a difference between expedient reasoning, here meaning secular reasoning that ends in conventional choices and right reasoning that pursues a higher good. Aristotle says the expediency of the good citizen, for example the driver who obeys all traffic rules does not make him a moral person. The moral person chooses a good act for its own sake such as would the driver who obeys traffic rules mainly due to his concern for the safety of others. On the other hand the temperate self-controlled man, the expedient good citizen reasons that the supreme good in behavior is moderation, let us say, in tactile pleasure (*Ex Ethic 1273*). He refrains due to convention. Moderation is considered by Aquinas a *quasi* principle of action. But the virtuous man, who has the right estimation of the end, apprehends the supreme good and the true principle of action. That estimation extends to a deeper appreciation of the value of another person and their wishes, the reason for the virtuous man placing limits on tactile pleasure. Love always respects someone's autonomy and dignity.

Aristotle obviously did not distinguish acquired virtue—the result of reason, from infused virtue that is the gift of the Holy

---

[11] See Ana Marta Gonzalez. *Depositum Gladius non Debet Restitui Furioso: Precepts, Synderesis, and Virtues in Saint Thomas Aquinas,* The Thomist. 63 (1999).

Spirit. Therefore, he refers to different levels of acquired virtue in distinguishing the *quasi* principles of action of the temperate man from the supreme good targeted by the man of virtue. Albeit on a naturally acquired level of reasoning Aristotle and Aquinas agree that knowledge of general moral principles and those principles that specify the greater good of acts [however limited] are within our grasp [Aristotle's profound insights is why Aquinas calls him the Philosopher].

There is a tendency—due to the aversion of acknowledging an ordered universe—toward making intended ends of acts the deciding principles of ethics. Visions of good results in areas such as the elimination of poverty, the alleviation of physical suffering, the promotion of class rights are made the end to the diminution of the means to the end of ethics. That is to say that the end justifies the means. The result is relativity in respect to actions because, as said the act is then measured by the degree of good or bad of the effect. A good act on the other hand should have a good effect. However, as seen above the resulting effect cannot determine whether the act is itself good or evil if we hold that there are acts that are either good or evil by nature. No one can reasonably argue that murder is justified in protecting our society. Nonetheless nations have murdered innocent persons for the assumed good of the nation and have claimed that such killing was not murder. Relativity in ethics is a form of selective reasoning. Bertrand Russell's ethical reasoning is an example. During his debate on the existence of God with Jesuit scholar Frederick Copleston he made the analogy, in reference to morality, of a jaundiced person who sees all things yellow. Russell's analogy assumes that what one feels at the time determines good and evil and not what is good and evil. Notwithstanding one's jaundiced view the fact is that good and evil are complete opposites and not similarities such as different hues of color. That discernment of opposites differs from pragmatic societal rules of behavior such as permissions and prohibitions that are subject to change. Russell's analogy of color does not address that distinction. That discernment is the interior conviction that this is good and that its violation is evil. Otherwise the judgment that separates moral good and evil from pragmatic rules, which can occasionally be legally transgressed, could not take place. But Russell's strong condemnations of war and injustice admit to evil. What we find in Bertrand Russell's thought is not the absence of moral judgment but selectivity.

The coherency of good in acts is in its convertibility with being. Evil requires the removal of good for its identification. It is the willful deprivation of some universal standard of justice, the taking of an inviolable right that belongs to another. Ethics as the pursuit of good assumes an entirely different dimension than acting out of self-interest. It targets what is best. The supreme good is not an ideal insofar as it is identified externally within standards of justice. We find its expression in acts invested for the good of another. The kind of love that flows from pursuit of a supreme good in acts possesses its own value. Does that make the supreme good an ontological reality apart from its identification with the practical end of an act? That certainly cannot be ruled out. A truth may be perceived clearly only on the natural level as ends of acts. Nevertheless apprehension of good on any level, because of its fluid nature anticipates something greater—like Saint Anselm's argument for the existence of God as that which nothing greater can be thought—compels us to explore the possibility of its being. Anselm's argument is more an appeal to faith and belief in God. It has value. Rational evidence however is thereafter better placed in exploration of the causality and hierarchy of being as we find in Aquinas' *Essence and Existence*.

Pursuit of the supreme good in acts objectifies good. Anyone who pursues good for its own sake envisions a good that transcends exigent need and practicality. Mohandas Gandhi did not overtly claim belief in a divinity, at least not in the Christian sense. He did exhibit mores whose object was of a transcendent nature and he articulated a sense of good that surpassed limited expedient reasoning. The transition from there to the existence of a personal deity that is love itself is of course a leap of faith. But this indicates that the love of good implies a form of reasoned faith and desire.

Ethical thought begins with the identification of good in the fullness of a thing's existence (*ST Ia2ae 94, 2*). Being is the source of good because God is the First Principle of all things. All things are created good and it is in beings that we first perceive good. Since the nature of moral good is to promote a being's integrity rather than deprive it of what is vital to its well-being, good then is a reality that is convertible to being. That is because ultimately in God alone essence is identical with existence (*ST Ia 3, 4*). God, whose essence is good, is the supreme good and First Principle of all existence (*De Ente 7, 43*). And by participation in his being all creatures share in his good. Yet it is only through the moral life as Boethius [Manlius Severinus] says that we share by participation in that supreme good that is God's essence. Through right reason we perceive all the goods that complete human nature. We see in this a commensurate relationship between our humanness and ethics.

The good had been declared by Aristotle as that which all men desire. There is in the will a rational dynamic toward the supreme good that is found in the desire to know. It is a reasoned desire for the source of goodness (*Virt Cmn 10, Ad 1*). The intellect has a natural desire to know truth (*ST Ia2ae 94, 2 Ad 2*). A desire however is motivated by something known. We perceive good in things that are good. But what makes the will desire what is not known since the supreme good is a perfection that transcends what is known? There is in the will a likeness to what is desired. It is anticipatory of our desire to know God. Man was created for that end. As there is the power to recognize charity in human acts there is the desire to know the source of good. Reason motivated by desire aims at a real intelligible. It is real since charity is the essence of God. As the Apostle John says where there is charity there is God. By faith in Christ who is the personification of charity we make the correlation to the supreme good in God.

The mind's natural tendency is to form universal concepts of truths that it discerns in the particular such as acts. It is always in the context of many particular instances and variable conditions of what is considered just that a universal sense of justice is formed. An example is the invariable constituents of a just wage that form a universal standard. These constituents would include remuneration proportionate to the service rendered and maintaining an acceptable standard of living. This tendency to form universal ideas of some good is called speculative reason as compared to practical reason. Practical reason then, which always considers ethical behavior in an actual event, deliberates the perceived details of a proposed action in order to determine and carry out the correct action in that given instance.

Reason is clearly the pathway to truth. Nevertheless we form views that are influenced by existential need, by philosophy, religion, and politics. However our criteria may lead to moral choices that conflict with the teachings of Christ and the Church. The controversy in ethics then is historically centered on that which makes an act good or evil. Aquinas addresses the ethical criteria of actions in *ST Ia2ae 18 On Good and Evil in Acts*. As indicated above he asserts that the *object* of the act, as well as circumstances and intent must all be correct. Object in one sense can be the physical recipient of a chosen act such as this person. Although all such objects, created beings, are good in themselves, not all acts are appropriate for a given object (*ST Ia2ae 18, 2 Ad 1*). For example, sexual activity is never appropriate with a child. Although the desire or even the intent for sexual activity of itself is not evil in such a case the agent's choice of object determines that the act is evil. But if sexual activity between an adult male and female, which by nature is licit, is nevertheless evil, as in adultery, prostitution, promiscuity then the object of the act is clarified as to its actual meaning. Object is the material species, which determines the kind of moral act it is in the manner that is similar to its form (*ST Ia2ae 18, 2 Ad 2*). Here the matter is not the child itself, a good, or an adult person, a good, but the *materia circa quam*, that which the act is about. The focus here is on the exterior act of the will, the choice of action. The principles of being, form and matter are applied by Aquinas to the act [an act is a movement from potency to actualization similar to the dynamics of created being], form in respect to intent and matter in respect to act. The internal act of the will is the intent, which gives the act its formal species. The object of the exterior act of the will is the matter by which the act is informed (*ST Ia2ae 18, 6*). There is unity in the formal and material species of an act insofar as intent and choice cannot be separated in respect to the morality of the will. The means to the end and the intent constitute a single object of the will since the means to the end are willed for sake of the end (*ST Ia2ae 12, 4 Ad 2*). The *moral object*, a terminology applied in contemporary ethics consequently must include the intention as it is expressed in the choice of act. That is why object gives the act its moral definition, since the faculties of the soul are ordered to their proper object, the object of the act itself (*ST Ia2ae 18, 7*). The object of a virtuous act is the realization of its proximate end. The perfection of the virtue fortitude, for example, is not a moral absolute but rather the proximate end as identified in the mean of fortitude, which is the demarcation between audacity and terror. Fortitude is the likeness of that moral habit impressed upon the action. We become what we do insofar as moral acts define our personality.

Virtue in Aristotle's *Ethic* begins with desire for some good, an end of nature, and prudence, the reasoned assessment of that desire. To desire something is to some degree to will it. The rational dimension of the human will includes understanding of the object of desire. Hence the will we saw is called the rational appetite. But if ends of nature are the initial good we desire the rational appetite also seems to determine the means to that end. Aristotle seems to presume that. The end of nature would then become the rule of rectitude for the intellect. Aquinas perceived the dilemma of a vicious circle that makes reason subject to desire, here the rational appetite. According to Aristotle's schematization we are back to square one. But choice can only follow the rational judgment of what is right or wrong. Aquinas' formula is at the heart of his ethics because it isolates the judgment of reason regarding the act as the final moral determinant. It also underlines the nature of that judgment as the apprehension of the correct action. It informs conscience and sets the conditions for freedom of choice. This specific sequence is frequently misjudged in ethics and has led to confusion in moral decision making since the proposed action, the judgment of reason, is indeed a principle of action, the all important apprehension of the singular principle. Aquinas' schema is a major contribution to moral decision making.

> The truth of practical reason is determined by its conformity to a correct appetitive faculty, whereas the truth that is the conclusion of practical reasoning in respect to the *means to the end* is the rule of rectitude for the appetite (*Sent Ethic 1139a27* Translation is mine).

Reason, not the rational appetite, determines the correct means to the end. The text indicates that the intellect has the capacity to apprehend good in the act itself, which act is a first principle possessing self-evident intelligibility.

The major premise [the universal] of the operative syllogism is not the final cause of knowledge of the means to the end. In fact the only necessity in deliberation concerns the conditions of the act (*ST Ia2ae 13, 6 Ad 2*). That assessment and correct choice of act isolates the object. What was reconsidered as morally good by choice of the appetitive faculty in *Sent Ethic 1139a22* is the end of nature. The sequence following deliberation of means to that end begins with the judgment of practical reason. That judgment of reason is the apprehension of the correct end of the action, a singular principle that differs from the end of nature. Following the judgment of reason prudence issues a command (*ST 2a2ae 52, 2*).

> Choice is the appetitive faculty deliberating, consequently it is a principle of action, and so of motion, i.e., in the manner of an efficient cause but not for the sake of something, i.e., in the manner of a final cause (*Cm Ethic 1133*).

The appetitive faculty is the efficient but remote cause in deliberating the conclusion. Hence choice for the appetitive faculty is simply "concern" for the means to the end. Final causality in determining the means to the end belongs to reason (*Sent Ethic 1139a31*). Choice of action follows what reason has judged (*ST Ia2ae 13, 1 Ad 2*). This prior assent of the intellect in judgment is essential to the sentient consent of the will (*ST Ia2ae 15, 2 Ad 1*). Although judgment, and command, presupposes an act of the will, the choice of the will that is concern for the end in deliberation is not "free judgment". Free judgment has a more concise role in respect to the intellect.

> Judgment is the conclusion of the counseling process. The course is determined first by a proposition of the reason, second by its acceptance by appetite, whence Aristotle says that *having formed our judgment through the process of counsel we desire what we have decided.* (*ST Ia 83, 3 Ad 2*).

Aquinas therefore distinguishes that choice of the appetitive faculty that correlates with deliberation and precedes rational judgment, from that choice that follows discernment and the judgment of the intellect, that is the free choice [free judgment] of an act to be done. Reason and will correspond in the identification of truth *but not necessarily in adherence to the truth.* Responsibility for our actions requires that antecedent cooperation of reason and will which constitute an informed conscience. Free choice of good or evil however must be the act of a conscience informed by judgment. If that were not so the command that proceeds from prudence and the choice that follows would not have relevance.

Reason and will cooperate closely at the outset of deliberation. Implied in discursive reason is choosing to follow one path to another. Nonetheless knowledge is actualization of the intellect in apprehension. Apprehension of the singular, the act that is the conclusion of counsel, and choice must remain distinct. Key to that separation is appreciation of the discursive process of reason as compared to apprehension. That distinction cannot be overlooked because the middle term of the practical intellect, as seen above, is that apprehension which links the predicate and subject of the conclusion. As to universal principles they are *per se notae*, self-evident principles that are likewise immediate and without need of a mediating middle term. But the middle term in the practical intellect is not reasoning guided by the will but apprehension of the singular, which is immediate and self-evident (*ST Ia 86, 1 Ad 2*). If there is no self-evident apprehension of a singular principle of action then the conclusion of counsel becomes what is desired, which is to return to the vicious circle addressed by Aquinas. As such deliberation would be rendered futile. What Aquinas in effect is saying is that reason is a process that must end with the apprehension of a principle, the proposed action.

Aquinas places morality in acts in which good and evil is discerned according to the act's conditions. This doctrine offers the most comprehensible structure available for that discernment. Judgment is a confirmation of that which is by its own nature good as ordained by God. A structure can be theoretical or it can be practical. The order of things as we perceive them in the world is our practical knowledge of the good. That good can be an appreciation of the nature of something, and what is vital to a thing's existence. Good is seen in things. Moral good is specified in and inferred from human acts.

A good act has a rational structure that complies with our practical reason. It is plain to see, for example, that offering someone stranded in the desert a lift is a good thing. What I do in that instance is intended for a good purpose because the decision to give a ride and leave them off safely benefits that person. However, when we perform an act that kills even with the consent of the person being killed we are faced with a dilemma. The withdrawal of life support under some conditions is killing, for example if withdrawn from a basically sound person when requiring it is a temporary measure. But if injecting someone with a lethal agent were not an act of killing under all conditions, then we are faced with another more encompassing dilemma—that of determining what an act of killing is. If such a death dealing procedure were determined to be medical care in some cases, then neither could we determine that withdrawal of life support in some cases is killing. That is because killing would not depend on the act but on the intent. Assessment of the conditions provides the act's object. If the standard for lethal care were a terminal condition, mental handicap, severe pain, and so forth then the presumption would be that killing is justified under these conditions. Quality of life would be the principal ethical standard. Even if we were to narrow the standards to terminal condition and severe pain, the standards would be challenged to include many other conditions including those that are not terminal. But most important and underlying the slippery slope argument is the act itself. If killing in medicine is sanctioned under some conditions then killing cannot be considered evil.

An example of the difference between killing and medical care is given in one of the earlier declarations demarcating the difference between what the Church considers ordinary treatment from extraordinary treatment. The terminology is based on what Orville Griese terms "ethically extraordinary."[12] This refers to the spiritual and emotional burden some treatments pose to the patient. Griese applies ethically extraordinary in place of extraordinary means, the latter referring to technology. Today much technology that was once considered extraordinary, such as respirators, is now

[12] Rev. Msgr. Orville N. Griese, STD, JCD. Director of Research, Pope John Center. *Catholic Identity in Health Care: Principles and Practice.* Braintree, MA: The Pope John Center, 1987. p. 160.

routinely used. However, the moral difficulties remain. The procedure may be an excessive physical and emotional burden for the long term and otherwise terminal patient. It also may prove an emotional burden for next of kin, and a burden on their resources. In such cases removal of the respirator at the patient's request is not suicide. The conditions of the act do not characterize a suicidal act because the cause of death is the pathology of the illness and not the removal of life saving treatment.

As early as 1957 Pius XII, in a limited forum, set forth principles for ethics that ran contrary to the thought of his contemporaries. Excessive burden can be emotive and even cultural. The statement recognizes cultural differences as possible conditions for assessing burden.

> First, does one have the right, or is one even under the obligation, to use modern artificial-respiration equipment in all cases, even those which, in the doctor's judgment, are completely hopeless. But normally one is held to use only ordinary means – according to circumstances of persons, places, times and culture – that is to say, means that do not involve any grave burden for oneself or another.[13]

Discernment can be affected by conditions such as tradition and indigenous mores. But obviously the good or evil nature of the act cannot be changed.

The inability to distinguish cause of death from the occasion of death precipitated by the withdrawal of life support has led to the errors of euthanasia and a physician assisted suicide. Charles Curran's position is an example. He sanctioned euthanasia on the basis that relief from suffering for a terminal patient justifies a

---

[13]Pius XII, *Address to International Congress of Anesthesiologists*. November 24, 1957.

"positive act of interfering" that is morally indistinguishable from the removal of life support.[14] Nevertheless if we blur that distinction it would follow that there is no distinction between acts of killing and the refusal of medical treatment or its withdrawal if it simply prolongs suffering and death. In other words killing becomes possible on the grounds of a good goal. This is the position later adopted by the proponents of physician-assisted suicide, who do not recognize the difference between removal of life support under reasonable conditions and euthanasia for the terminally ill. Pius XII clarified such a right of the patient to refuse medical technology if there is spiritual burden.

> A more strict obligation would be too burdensome for most men and would render the attainment of higher, more permanent good too difficult. Life, health, all temporal activities are in fact subordinated to spiritual ends.[15]

On the other hand withholding nutrition and hydration to permanently comatose patients unless it poses a burden is immoral. Nutrition and hydration is comfort care. Unlike the respirator used for pulmonary function that is permanently compromised the digestive system of the comatose patient functions but he suffers the handicap of inability to ingest. The Congregation for the Doctrine of the Faith since the address of Pius XII has recognized the extension of ethics to burden as perceived by the patient.

---

[14] Charles E. Curran, *The Principle of Double Effect: Some Historical and Contemporary Observations.* Atti Congresso Internazionale. D/5. April, 1974. p. 449.

[15] Pius XII, *Address to International Congress of Anesthesiologists*. November 24, 1957.

> One cannot impose on anyone the obligation to have recourse to a technique which is already in use but which carries a risk or is *burdensome.* Such a refusal is not the equivalent of suicide; on the contrary, it should be considered as an acceptance of the human condition, or a wish to avoid the application of a medical procedure disproportionate to the results which can be expected, or a desire not to impose excessive expense on the family or community.[16]

The line between good medical care and euthanasia may not always be clear because of the many variables involved. Discernment of the evil of euthanasia is in the conditions that are evident to us. Reason and the laws of nature confirm what our intellect apprehends. Reason does not manufacture the truth, as we find when truth is rationalized. It discovers it. Reason is the measure but not the rule of what is true (*ST Ia2ae 91, 3 Ad 2*). Murder then is evidently evil by its very nature.

The recurrent difficulty with discerning moral truth in the delivery of medical care is that the criteria are not always that visible. The object of the act may seem less clear when medical procedures such as craniotomy are applied to remove an infant lodged in the mother's birth canal. Ethicists have argued that the procedure when applied, as a last resort to remove the infant and at least save the mother's life is not killing. Others will argue that it is reprehensible because it abrogates the oath taken by the medical profession to do no harm. A craniotomy that crushes the infant's skull is an act designed to kill the infant. But proponents of the procedure say the craniotomy is intended to modify the infant's dimensions in order to remove it from the birth canal. If the act is designed to kill the object of the act is to kill. A viable resolution

[16] *Declaration on Euthanasia. Sec. IV. 1980*, Sacred Congregation for the Doctrine of the Faith.

is in procedures not designed to kill albeit at the risk of losing the infant or mother. Perhaps the best procedure in cases of obstructed labor is the caesarean section.[17] This procedure having a possible double effect avoids the intentional death of either. And it would provide a response to the hypothetical often posed by pro choice advocates that abortion is sometimes necessary to save the life of the mother. The more important issue then is that neither the intention of the act or its object is meant to kill.

Medical procedures cannot employ instruments of death. The conundrum posed in using a procedure that has the direct purpose of killing is the validation of killing as medical treatment. Moral theologians have traditionally associated responsibility with the choice of act. That refers to the theological concept of who wills the means also wills the end known as voluntarium in causa. In the latter instance, the method employed is not merely the *occasion* of death, but the *cause* of death.[18] When it is evident that an act is designed to kill we cannot disassociate the choice of act from the object of the act for the same reason that we cannot disengage good intent from choice of evil acts. We are judged by what we do even if our intentions appear to be for a greater good. Aquinas addresses the heart of the matter when he says that a man becomes abominable to God because of the evil he does (*ST Ia2ae 18, 2*).

Much of the growing controversy regarding euthanasia rests on the inability of many, including physicians, to make the distinction, as delineated by Orville Griese between occasion of death and

---

[17] This was the first recommendation given by Carmen Dolea M.D. and Carla AbouZahr M.D. to the World Health Organization held at Geneva in 2003. The next unfortunate recommendation was the abortive use of forceps.

[18] Msgr. Orville N. Griese. *Conserving Human Life.* Braintree, MA: The Pope John XXIII Medical-Moral Research and Educational Center, 1989. pp. 159-160.

cause of death. The basic principle is that if the underlying permanent illness will cause death without permanent medical intervention such as life support then the illness is the cause of death and not the removal or withholding of medical care. However that principle has to be validated by other conditions. Validating conditions are that delivery of this kind of medical care benefits the patient and does not pose an ethically extraordinary burden.

Peter Abelard is known for an approach to ethical questions, which is not far removed from contemporary thought opposed to locating morality in the choice of act. Abelard believed in a hierarchy of reasoned principles. He argued that universal truths are supreme and that ethics pursue what is universally true. Consequently an act is not good or evil in itself. A host of present day ethicists say the same. Abelard added that the intent of the will, some universal good, determines the good or evil of an act. He said it is not the physical action or an assumed injury to God that is sinful. Only acting in formal contempt of God is sinful.

The first point of Abelard's mistaken assumptions is God does not determine good and evil. The next is that sin is exclusive to consciously wishing to offend God. Man simply requires the intention to bring about some greater good. Abelard's view regarding evil is misdirected psychology. Acts from his ethical perspective have no value. But the truth is that an act is evil insofar as it does an injustice to someone. Man albeit Abelard or anyone else does not define justice. God does. A malicious disposition toward anyone is evil and offends God.

The basic premise of Abelard's thought nonetheless remains popular. Add to this the view among progressives that man's independent reasoning is a fuller participation in the creative act, and a more complete realization of his humanity. Accordingly ethical thought is assumed to be a more prolific understanding of compassion, and outcomes that benefit all. Max Scheler's totality of the good and one's inner feelings of good and evil is said to have contributed to this approach. That opinion of Scheler who sought to return ethics to experience is debatable.[19] When advocates of ethical proportionalism proposed that the intent of the will in given circumstances determines the good or evil of an act John Paul II addressed the dynamic of intent in a human act.

> The reason why a good intention is not itself sufficient, but a correct choice of actions is also needed, is that the human act depends on its object, whether that object is *capable or not of being ordered* to God, to the One who "is alone good", and thus brings about the perfection of the person.[20]

That mirrors Aquinas' view that the ultimate end is found in the means to the end. There are acts that are good according to their species and are brought about through acquired virtue. But for man to reach his or her ultimate end acquired virtue is insufficient. A correct choice of act, whatever it may be, must be capable of being ordered to God. There are acts that cannot be otherwise. What does that mean? Well, it is easy enough to imagine acts that are good in themselves such as giving a stranded person a lift. Intent and choice here are virtually indistinguishable. Can such an act be ordered to the supreme good? Presumably, if the intent is charitable it is. But someone who does the same through a naturally acquired sense of virtue available to all also does good. But who is to judge whether acts of that kind conform to charity

---

[19] See Benedict M. Ashley, OP. Kevin D. O'Rourke, OP. *Health Care Ethics. 4th ed.* Washington, D.C.: Georgetown University Press, 1997. p. 160.
[20] John Paul II. *Veritatis Splendor*, 78.

except God who sees the heart of man? Then there are complex acts, which are distinguished not simply by intent but by multiple intent and choice. Those are acts, which remain definable by the object of the act. If someone were to have a child out of wedlock and raised it despite the opprobrium of her neighbors it might appear to be an act conformable to charity. But she may have decided to keep the child because her lover offered her a handsome sum. Otherwise she would have exposed the infant to the elements—even today infants are found in dumpsters. That is an act in which the interior object of the will, intent, is not so pure. The external object, insofar as keeping the infant warm and healthy, is good. The object of the act suffers morally because of the poor motivation to raise the infant. The external object of the will can appear good and from all outward appearances the object of the act is good. Unfortunately appearances are not what reveal the true object and moral species of the act. The person's less than charitable motivation is the actual object of the act, *that which the act is about.* An act in order to be good must be good as well as be seen to be good (*ST Ia2ae 19, 6*).

In summary morality depends on the act as well as the will. If good or evil were entirely dependent on the intent of the will then intention could determine that an evil such as murder would be good. The external act of the will is choice and refers to the proximate end within the act. That proximate end, the discovery of the virtuous mean is the judgment of reason.

> The goodness or malice which the external action has of itself, on account of its being about due matter and its being attended by due circumstances, is not derived from the will but by reason. Consequently, if we consider the goodness of the external action in so far as it comes from reason's ordering and apprehension, it is prior to the act of the will (*ST Ia2ae 20, 1*).

Reason judges the act prior to willing. Choice follows. A human action "is right or sinful by reason of its being good or evil" (*ST Ia2ae 21, 1*). The proximate end of an act of virtue must be entirely good because every privation of a good in any subject is an evil (*ST Ia2ae 21, 2*).

Clearly discernment of an objective order is the ground of ethics. While acts are directed by nature to specific ends, such as man's natural desire for sustenance, acts are determined by reason in respect to the correct means to the end. Aquinas uses the Latin *ea quae sunt ad finem*, the means to the end primarily as the act. As shown he differentiates the act's own end, its object from the person's intent. Aquinas understandably continues to emphasize throughout his works that morality is centered in the act's object, what it does and not simply by the intent.

Aquinas opens his discussion on good and evil in human acts in *ST Ia2ae 18* by specifying that the good is found in its compliance with the fullness of being (*ST Ia2ae 18, 1*). Moral evil as said is the willful deprivation of an inviolable good belonging to a being. It is not strictly the absence of good. It is a practical assessment of the nature of good and evil. The absence of good is first of all physical evil. An example would be the inequality of the possession of goods. It does not mean that if someone owns property, and someone who lacks property suffers because of the lack, that the owner is morally responsible for the latter's travail. The same holds true in respect to the inequality of salaries. A person may be more gifted and possess better credentials than another and deserving of greater compensation. Some persons work harder than others who are just as fit. Absence does not always indicate injustice. Moral evil requires there be some willed deprivation of that which rightfully belongs to another. A just wage then is a moral as well as legal right. And if someone has the means and is aware of another in serious need there is moral obligation to assist. That should not be based on justice in the strict judicial sense but on the freedom to exercise charity, which is at the heart of justice. Governments that enforce exaggerated policies of equal distribution violate justice by denying deserved compensation for exceptional service, inhibit entrepreneurship, personal charity, and thus degrade society. Religious who freely share material goods in common instead practice mutual love.

While absence of physical good is a form of evil, and can have moral ramifications, the integrity of being, particularly a person's being then is the focal point for Aquinas in the determination of moral good and evil. Since an act's good is similarly found in its compliance with the fullness of being the first condition for ethical analysis of a human act is that it be understood as a complete act. All the constituents of a human act correspond to being. Just as intent and choice cannot be separated from the morality of the person neither can intent and choice be considered apart from their impact on the object (*ST Ia2ae 18, 1*). The object is different from the person's intent. What we intend is not what the act actually does. For example I cause a person's death by lethal injection with the intent of ending their suffering. In utilitarian ethics the act is the means to achieve the intent. The utilitarian would reverse the ancient principle that the end does not justify the means by saying it does. But the correct means to the end doctrine refers to a singular principle that is an apprehension separate from but corresponding to knowledge of the universal. Its recognition ensures the practice of ethics centered on virtue expressed in acts rather than on the assumed good outcomes of utilitarianism. Utilitarianism does not center on the mean in deliberation of an act whereas the virtuous mean is not excessive or defective.

> Prudence advances with the apprehension of two principles. One is knowledge of the universal, which knowledge is within the intellect's capacity and is acquired naturally; and is not simply speculative but practical knowledge, such as do no evil. The other apprehension is, as noted in the *Ethics*, the knowledge of an ultimate, a first principle that is the principle of action within the contingent world (*ST 2a2ae 49, 2 Ad 1.* Translation is mine).

Some ask to what extent, may a moral principle *override* another. Overriding refers to comparing universals as if by so doing the correct act can be determined. An example is the comparison of the principle of human dignity, when quality of life is compromised to the principle of sanctity of life. The error is it may be presumed that preserving human dignity instead of life better serves the patient. Euthanasia then changes from killing to an act of mercy. To avoid this error Aquinas ensures the integrity of the act by subjecting it to deliberation and the scrutiny of the principles of the natural law.

As the divinity is sovereign so is the right to life of men, women, children, and infants in the womb all of whom by nature reflect the divinity. That right is inviolable from conception to death regardless of perceived quality of life. The principles of right to life and sanctity of life are increasingly abrogated on the basis of deformity and handicap. While physicians and ethics committees may find instances when care seems futile and the request for that care unreasonable that right must never be removed from the patient or infant in the womb. That right is given by God and not by the state or any committee assuming such authority.

Another approach is the *preferential utilitarianism* of Princeton ethicist Peter Singer. In *Practical Ethics* Singer advocates the killing of handicapped infants yet to develop rationality. Singer declares that equal justice based on sanctity of human life is religious belief. He then reasons if our killing of animals [Singer was originally an animal rights advocate] is justified on the basis of man's higher degree of intelligence, then persons who lack intelligence due to infancy, or handicap such as age or retardation should be subject to the same rules. His rationale for killing humans is to end the suffering of the handicapped, and to use the means available to end that suffering, with the consent of patient or proxy. From his perspective the question of means to the end, the morality of the act itself, is equivocation. This makes the intended outcome the criteria for moral judgment and mitigates the distinction between medical care and murder. For Singer and others if the good physical effect sufficiently outweighs the evil physical effect then the act is justified. [21] Morality once again becomes intention. What is lost in this is the true meaning of ethics, which is about the choice of good or evil acts.

Circumstances are criteria that can change the moral complexion of a situation. Although they are considered accidental to the act they can affect its nature. Circumstances may be selected to do damage. A physician receives a confidential message to be given exclusively to another physician. Instead of relaying it privately he announces it publicly to embarrass him. Karl Rahner also held circumstances can alter the nature of an act but perhaps in a different sense, seeming to imply circumstances may favorably affect the morality of an otherwise evil act. We consequently should consider "the circumstances surrounding this type of case as something absolutely individual" and that it is an "absolutely unique case."[22] Although circumstances may make an otherwise

---

[21] Philosopher Peter Unger of New York University is quoted as saying "he's the most influential ethicist alive" in the *President's Page*, Princeton Weekly Bulletin December 7, 1998.

good act evil, they cannot transform an evil act into a good one. Neither can effects make a good act evil or an evil act good (*ST Ia2ae 18, 2*). An action *ordered* to a good effect is a good action. The actual outcome does not alter that. Abortion is killing not because of the evil material effect of the infant's death, which can be accidental but that the act is intended to kill. A well-intended surgery may accidentally end in the death of an infant. It is either the intention to commit evil or the choice of means to do evil that makes an act evil. Aquinas makes it clear in *ST 2a2ae 64, 7* that effects are in the realm of physical good and physical evil. Moral evil is always in the will.

An act however is considered good to the extent that it can produce a good effect. That means that it must be ordered to a good effect. "Consequently the very proportion of an action to its effect is the measure of its goodness" (*ST Ia2ae 18*, *2 Ad 3*). For it to be proportionate to a good effect it must be ordered to that according to all the ethical criteria as noted of a good act: good object, circumstances, and intent. That includes the interior as well as the external objects of the will. Insofar as the act is so proportioned it is good. Nevertheless an act may not achieve the desired effect since at times that is dependent on transient conditions which the agent of the act does not always control. For example, one may will good for another by doing some service and the person for whom it was done may respond negatively. A well planned construction project may have poor results due to unforeseen variables. The actual outcome does not make the act evil. The act itself is good to the degree that it is proportioned, i.e. executed to a good effect.

---

[22] Karl Rahner, in *Das Dynamische*, quoted by William Wallace, O.P. in *Existential Ethics: A Thomistic Appraisal,* The Thomist. 27 (1963). p. 506.

What this all means is that because we know what is good in general, which are the general principles of the natural law, we can identify it in particulars, which are acts. If we can do that we can draw up a formal syllogism with a middle term. If helping the poor is charitable, and providing shelter to transients is helping the poor, then providing shelter to transients is charitable. The act of providing shelter to the poor to meet the standard of charity must fulfill all the conditions that define charity. Is this person poor? Is the shelter adequate? Apart from a hypothetical, which is all a formal syllogism gives us, the actual act is subject to assessment and the scrutiny of the principles of the natural law, which the natural retention by the intellect as said is called *synderesis.*

The term *synderesis* was applied by Saint Gregory Nazianzen to indicate the function of the practical intellect, the intellect engaged in assessing acts within the principles of natural law. In turn the definitive feature of human nature is the inherent ability to apprehend good and practice it. Nevertheless moral evil may occur if there is formal consent to acts that are evil regardless of external action (*De Ver 15, 4*). Principles exist at both ends of the spectrum of an act. First the ends of nature and knowledge of the general principles of the natural law, and at the other end the means to the end that specify natural law.

> "The light of Your countenance, O Lord, is signed upon us"; [Ps. 4: 6] thus implying that the light of natural reason, whereby we discern what is good and what is evil, which pertains to the natural law, is nothing else but an imprint on us of the divine light. It is therefore evident that the natural law is nothing else than the rational creature's participation of the eternal law (*ST Ia2ae 91, 2*).

Natural law speaks to the natural inclination in us to perceive the proper end and act. That natural inclination directed by reason to its proper act is moral virtue. Prudence, right reason in human acts, is synonymous with moral virtue. We cannot have one, that is, prudence, without moral virtue, or conversely, we cannot have moral virtue without prudence. Moral virtue is a disposition to will rightly as well as reason rightly. Moral virtue is what provides perspicacity regarding the morality of our actions.

The rational process of identifying the structure of the natural law is creative. Contrary to what some commentators assume the person engaged in practical reason is not simply identifying facts in nature. The person assumes a creative relationship with the object. That is because discernment of what is good leaves the imprint of the self on the act (*ST Ia2ae 93, 5*). It is an impression that enhances the person who acts virtuously by his or her becoming virtuous. The act reaches its perfection through the unique personality and charisms of the one who impresses it. Each person has his or her way of adding richness to a human act.

When the will is motivated by moral virtue the will cooperates with reason and its target becomes apparent. The virtuous person is disposed to act when the good is discerned. The spirituality of the person becomes evident. The eternal law is reflected in acts that are consistent with the order of nature.

3. ORDER

There is coherent direction of all things toward discernible ends. It is called natural law. Physical nature cannot direct itself as secularists argue it does since it cannot supersede its nature. That ultimate intelligent cause is the Creator Word who directs all things toward good ends. The eternal law is reflected in the order of nature. Behavior when morally correct corresponds to this permanent order. Man is given the intellect to discern that order and live by it, to apprehend the logic of the part from the whole, true and false, and good and evil. Reason therefore reveals a natural law in man, a prescient order of knowledge that guides social interaction. These are the general principles of the natural law that are known to all. It is the inherent capacity to distinguish good from evil.

Right reason is the rational compliance to the natural order in the exercise of liberty and the pursuit of happiness. Even those addicted to the pleasures of life must to some degree comply within these parameters. Otherwise they exclude themselves as sociopaths. Lucretius the advocate of pleasure wrote, "Such is the power of reason to overcome inborn vices that nothing prevents our living a life worthy of the gods" (*Proem 3.321-22*).

The anthropology of Aquinas begins with the premise that man is created good. We have a bent toward goodness that is integral to our human nature. But the presence of evil in the world seems an anomaly. Pain and suffering are evils. Evil in respect to human behavior is deeper and more complex. It often seems ambiguous. Ancient doctrines attempting to explain the anomaly of evil persist today in various forms. Zoroaster 6th century B.C. taught that evil is part of the order of nature and like good is an entity emanating from the divinity. Mani 2nd century A.D., another Persian initiated the widespread religious movement called Manichaeism. He similarly taught that good and evil are entity like forces in the universe. Yet Mani borrowed concepts from Christianity such as darkness standing for evil and light for good. He repudiated Jesus of Nazareth and alleged that the Canonic Gospels are daemonic. He instead preached an ethereal Cosmic Jesus, similar to New Age who does not suffer crucifixion but indicates the light within us. Saint Augustine was actually a Manichean prior to his conversion to the Jesus of Nazareth of Christianity. In John's Gospel Christ is the Light of the World that darkness cannot overcome. Augustine as a Christian convert describes evil as darkness that exists only in relation to the light of good. Aquinas as is often the case follows Augustine and says that evil if it is to exist at all must exist alongside good, that is, in reference to good. Evil then is not its own substance. It is not a thing but is a deviation from good. If we take into account that man's natural inclinations, are at the start always toward some good the tendency toward evil, which is a deviation from an ordered response to that good must involve a free act of the will. Evil is in the will.

While the nature of things such as this horse or this man is invariable what is good or evil may vary according to conditions. However the argument is made that if justice varies under some conditions then all matters of justice are subject to change. That position, although disputed by Aquinas may on first take seem reasonable. In support of it one may say it is not necessary to return a weapon belonging to someone bent on murder.[23] Clearly that is correct. The argument then deserves close scrutiny because it adversely impacts moral judgment. Example: it has been my

---

[23]Gonzalez, Ana Marta. *Depositum Gladius non Debet Restitui Furioso: Precepts, Synderesis, and Virtues in Saint Thomas Aquinas,* The Thomist. 63 (1999). p. 225.

experience that many physicians hold that if it is morally acceptable to remove the respirator from a patient dependent on it then so is physician assisted suicide. But the conditions differ. The object of the former is not to kill but to avoid the prolonged and unnecessary suffering of an otherwise terminal patient. Murder is always an injustice of the first order. Suicide is the same.

The issue centers on dealing with secondary principles derived from the nature of justice, such as ownership of property, civil laws, traditions related to marriage, and penalties for offences that led some to believe that justice itself was mutable. Aquinas clarifies that misconception saying that actions which belong to the very nature of justice are immutable. Murder, false witness, and suicide are always an injustice. Actions derived from the nature of justice are in some instances variable (*Sent Ethic 1134b24*).

> By stating that sin has a cause *per accidens*, and that the variable correctness of precepts of natural law ultimately depends on this cause *per accidens*, Aquinas excludes an essential mutation of the natural law, for the same reason he rules out an essential mutation of nature.[24]

The will has a natural propensity toward good. The cause of sin is incidental [*per accidens*] to the will because the choice to sin does not belong to the nature of the will. It is rather a deviation from it. Free choice therefore should not include any natural predilection in us to choose evil since God created man in His own image. Something evidently is missing from human nature that affects, if not the freedom of the will, a desultory leaning to commit evil. What is missing then is a filial relationship between man and God. Augustine's and Aquinas' response is original sin. Man in

[24] Gonzalez, *Depositum Gladius*, p. 227.

consequence is at odds with God and the order of his creation. Evil is described by Augustine and Aquinas as an act of the will that occurs when we knowingly deviate from that natural order. The supposition is that if evil is to exist there must be an order from which we willingly deviate. We are first aware of that order in our inclinations toward some good. The awareness of the pleasurable ends of our desires gives us the initial knowledge of what is called the natural law. They are what Aquinas calls the ends of nature.

ENDS OF NATURE AND ENDS OF ACTS

All animals desire pleasurable ends. This then is where man differs. The correct means to these natural ends require reason. Morality begins with reason and the discernment of the ends of acts. This rational consciousness of good and evil in actions is the very basis of the natural law within us. We draw our general knowledge of what is moral from our actions, which completes our knowledge of the natural law. Consequently conscience is formed by our knowledge of the ends of nature and our general knowledge of good behavior. The propensity in us toward good is what enables us to discern right from wrong. Awareness of right and wrong in acts while intellectual is self-evident similar to our immediate awareness of the good of ends of nature. Although reason by nature is inclined toward truth without the intellect's apprehension reason can also lead to very diverse views. The apprehension of good in acts therefore is definitive. It completes the reasoning process. There is not simply intelligence in man as in the sense of animal intelligence but rather an all encompassing and superior propensity that makes the human soul essentially different from all other creatures. That is the rationale of Albert the Great the mentor of Aquinas calling man not simply a rational animal but a moral animal. Man's intellect possesses the unique power of reflecting on what he perceives and the self that perceives. This self reflection allows man to recognize an interior propensity toward good in the act of apprehension. He is consequently certain of his apprehension. Reason then assists the intellect's capacity to apprehend the truth of our actions by confirming that the proposed act conforms to the principles of natural law. Reason leads us to truth and then offers further assurance of that truth. This reflective capacity of the intellect results in comprehension and certitude. This natural order of knowing within us mirrors the eternal order.

> All things emanate from the divine will, and each and every thing has its own distinctive appetite for goodness. So there must be one appetite that tends to goodness in general and is implied by reason; and another that tends to this or that particular good and implied by sensation (*ST Ia 59, 1*).

Reason ordered by nature to its proper object targets the truth about things. The first principle of the natural law to do good and avoid evil stems from this most basic inner motion of all living things toward life and goodness as opposed to death and evil. A predisposition toward good indicates there is potency that focuses our inclinations and enables us to discern good. It is primordial because it predates experience. As there is movement of a sensual nature toward a particular good end there is the rational propensity in us toward truth in acts from which general moral principles are formed. Discernment comes to completion with the process of assessment of the correct means to that end. Similarly ends of nature of the intellect such as the desire to know, the desire for success are assessed in respect to achieving those ends. This practical actualization of the power to discern good from evil is the preeminent moral virtue called prudence, which is defined as right reason in human acts. This natural predisposition has its scriptural basis in St. Paul. The law is *written in man's heart* (*Rm 2:15*).

Today the distinction between good and evil is often blurred. Many ethicists reject the existence of natural law. Their supposition is that exceptions prove there are no laws of nature. The blindness in this is the refusal to accept the necessity of actual laws for there to be exceptions to them. Free thought is touted to be the supreme arbiter of right and wrong. But it is reason without order, or at least the repudiation of order where adherence to it is inconvenient. Others propose, as do an increasing number of Catholic ethicists that the natural law written in man's heart is an interior knowledge that surpasses objective natural law principles. The controversy is addressed by ethicist Martin Rhonheimer in his critique of Joseph Fuchs' book *Natural Law*. On the one hand the natural law is correctly understood by Josef Fuchs as not merely the isolation of ends of nature but primarily as the reasoned ends of acts. Any animal as said may follow its instincts but only man assesses the truth of his actions. Reasoned acts define virtue and consequently ethics. However it is commonplace in a society given to individualism to hold that ethical judgments find viability within one's perspective. Rhonheimer describes Fuchs' version of natural law as a subjective exclusion of natural law principles. Norms drawn from our reasoned response to ends of nature are said by Rhonheimer to be wrongfully distinguished by Fuchs from "law" found "in the heart of man." [25] Nevertheless it is true that human nature is limited and superseded by the eternal law. And Fuchs will argue that this interior insight from the heart does not actually contradict natural law but simply surpasses it. Some make

---

[25] Martin Rhonheimer. *The Cognitive Structure of the Natural Law and the Truth of Subjectivity*, The Thomist. 67 (2003). p. 2.

the case that Fuchs' doctrine corresponds with the doctrine of moral object found in *Veritatis Splendor.* For many others the dilemma raised by Fuchs is that moral judgment in the end is personal opinion. Are there then appropriate moral responses that simply surpass natural law? There are infused moral principles that surpass our natural capacity but do not contradict justice. And reasoned ends of acts are inviolable laws when definitive of the nature of justice.

If the natural law is simply a set of guidelines that are subject to modification then it is not law in the strict sense. But if natural law reflects eternal law then there are natural inclinations and desires that have unchangeable ends. We could hardly speak of human nature and explain what it means to be human unless there are inclinations that are determined to such specific ends. And it must always be understood that it is the specificity of good acts and not simply the capacity to make different choices that marks our humanness. The choice of evil degrades humanness.

Reason in compliance with the first principles of the natural law determines with absolute certitude that there are certain ends of nature that are themselves inviolable. Reason in such instances determines appropriate behavior in distinct consideration of them. For example the first natural principle of all living creatures is to maintain life. For man that end of nature is inviolable. Therefore from this natural end are derived moral principles that uphold the sanctity of human life and its transmission. Fuchs' understanding of contra-positions suggests the impossibility that the eternal law, which the natural law reflects is actually in opposition to revelation.[26] This is implied in Fuchs' distinction between the "Creator and the natural law" and "the Redeemer and Revelation".

---

[26] Josef Fuchs, S.J. *Natural Law.* Trans. by M. H. Gill and Sons Ltd. New York: Sheed and Ward, 1965. pp. 10-11.

It resembles Nestorius' mistaken doctrine of duality of persons in Christ, one divine and one human. Fuchs' doctrine separates natural law of the Creator Word from "soteriological love of the Redeemer."[27] A "law of love" in man's heart is set in opposition to natural law. A law of love in the heart of man that transcends the reasoned order of nature is, if opposed to definitive Church doctrine antithetical to truth. Moral principles that are the gift of the Holy Spirit and supersede man's natural abilities never conflict with *essential* Church doctrine. Feelings of love alone do not define morality. Sentient adherence to moral good begins with apprehension. Adherence is motivated by grace. Divine love motivates love whose object is confirmed by faith and reason.

Fuchs' position cannot confirm that what one does is moral. The essential difference in Aquinas' ethics is the ability to scrutinize proposed actions by inference back to the natural law and doctrine. Aquinas does not subject the natural law and the eternal law to an esoteric antagonism. He instead emphasizes that good is convertible to being (*ST Ia2ae 18, 3 Ad 3*). In so doing he provides us with an objective rational structure as the basis for certitude. The essential and inviolable integrity of a person's being is the objective ground for ethical assessment. Accordingly knowledge of ends of nature and the ability to rationally apprehend ends of acts are a natural potency in the heart of man. As such Aquinas presents us with a practical, non-esoteric means for discernment.

Evil is a willful deprivation of an inviolable good belonging to someone. And it is from the distinctive nature of man that standards of justice are inferred. Natural law ethics centers on the virtues justice and charity because justice resides in the decision to love our neighbor. That decision emulates the eternal law and true soteriological love.

---

[27] Fuchs. *Natural Law.* p. 167.

The rational assessment of the natural order determines morality, which is not subject to personal views and intuitionalism. Man is not the arbiter of truth, God is. That is evident in nature and especially in what is revealed. It corresponds with Bernard Lonergan's premise in *Insight* that the "good of order" is the root of ethics and that "the actual good is identical with actual intelligibilities and so includes but also may extend beyond human values."[28] Human values here are acquired moral principles and social convention. That which extends beyond according to Aquinas is the moral principles revealed to us by the Holy Spirit. Lonergan was correct insofar as he perceived that the intrinsic rational structure of good in nature is reflective of the divine order and the identification of truth with the supreme good.

The thematic notion of ordering acts to the supreme good is found in Aristotle and specified by Saint Thomas Aquinas as being ordered to God. This same theme of moral acts being necessarily being ordered to God is the main point of John Paul II in *Veritatis Splendor* in his explication of the object of an act. The theme, a vital truth discerned by those mentioned exemplifies the virtue of prudence, the implied reason being that human reason has its limitations. It is through the gifts of the Holy Spirit by which principles of action are infused that raise prudence to its true perfection. We find examples of this philosophical theological doctrine in the moral teaching on contraception in *Humanae Vitae* which transcended the repeated contrary opinion of a special commission called by the encyclical's author Pope Paul VI.

As said there are ends of nature such as the right to life that are for man inviolable. Nevertheless we may reason that in some instances there are exceptions. It was thought that a murderer

[28] Bernard Lonergan. *Insight*, London: Darton Longman and Todd, 1958. pp. 604-5.

forfeits the right to life and deserves the death penalty—as was the position of Saint Thomas Aquinas. The Church has since moved away from the death penalty. However the removal of specific freedoms from criminals by the justice system to reprimand and to protect society is universal. Then there is war and the right to kill the enemy. Many argue that war is evil. Nonetheless there is just war if a nation defends itself against attack. Even atrocity like genocide against a people by government or external power can be justification for intervention. Morally the strong including nations have a given obligation to protect the weak. Thus we have international law and accords like the Geneva Convention. The Church inspired by the Holy Spirit has the inherent right to legislate and has exercised it in defining the extension and limitation of moral laws in all spheres of life. The rights of men and nations are in the end determined by God and observed by our correct understanding of justice.

4. JUSTICE

The practice of justice is inseparable from natural law. That is because knowledge of the ends of nature are necessary in defining our rights and in consequence our humanness.

> For this reason justice has its own special proper object over and above the other virtues, and this object is called the just, which is the same as right. Hence it is evident that right is the object of justice (*ST 2a2ae 57, 1c*).

Productive discussion on the practice of this virtue invariably begins with identifying rights that we share in common. This should avoid flawed ideas such as that referred to by Alasdair MacIntyre as "sentiment that effects adherence to rules".[29] The problem pointed out in *After Virtue* is the changing conceptions of rules that define justice. The conversation has moved from individual justice that identifies a person's intrinsic rights to more transitory societal concepts. If we were to isolate a starting point for discussing man's inviolable rights then life should be the foremost value. From the premise of the convertibility of being with good we can accurately isolate standards of justice that follow, beginning with the right to life, human dignity, autonomy and so forth. Nevertheless the question is to what extent the good of society might override the rights of the individual. There are many just laws that protect the common good from overreaching individuals. On the other hand justice places the needs of the individual in extreme cases above the common rights of others.

---

[29] Alasdair MacIntyre. *After Virtue.* 2nd ed. London: Duckworth, 1987. p. 244.

> It is not theft, properly speaking, to take secretly and use another's property in a case of extreme need, because that which he takes for the support of his life becomes his own property by reason of that need (*ST 2a2ae 66*, *7 Ad 2*).

Rules address standards of justice as either inviolable or subject to modification. The right to private ownership can at times be modified in deference to the principle of the common good. As MacIntyre point out "To own something is not, as in some views, to have inviolable rights over it." [30]

A just society in this ethical framework is not necessarily a democracy but rather a body that first ensures the right to life of the innocent. Nationalists who executed civilians because they were Marxists were as guilty as Loyalists who murdered priests and nuns in civil war Spain. Although either side in the war claimed justification for some higher good it is the acts of murder that were unjust. And although as MacIntyre indicates there are changing conceptions of justice in politics and economics there are more permanent international law agreements, in particular the Geneva Convention that is intended to protect human dignity as well as the lives of captured combatants and innocent civilians. Violations of justice in the mistreatment of prisoners and detainees such as torture, humiliation, and sexual assault are recognized worldwide as inhuman and intolerable. That recognition is a universal affirmation of the inviolable principles of the right to life and human dignity that repudiates the frequent rationalizations of politicians. Human rights in the end must be drawn from our understanding of human nature. Standards of justice are precisely the observable rights that belong to man.

---

[30] Alasdair MacIntyre. *How Can We Learn What Veritatis Splendor Has To Teach*? The Thomist. 58 (1994). p. 180.

Ethics is practiced by society at large and most clearly distinguished in our laws. Human law is Aquinas' terminology for civil law. In the codification of civil laws governing human behavior we come to appreciate the rational basis of human nature. After all civil laws are the rational modification of human desires. Jurisprudence in America is primarily based on the Common Law of England. The Common law is referred to as the unwritten tradition of ecclesiastical law, natural law, reasoning, and custom, and is perceived in legal circles as "enlightened public policy."[31] It is in effect a common source of ethics. Abortion, for example, which had been traditionally prohibited by the Common Law, was wrongly adjudicated by the Supreme Court as a right. Jurists including former Chief Justice Rehnquist later argued that there is no evidence that meets the standards for such a right since it is not "deeply rooted in this Nations history and tradition" (*Moore v. East Cleveland, 431 U.S. 494, 1997*). Rehnquist wisely applies the term human life when he speaks of its purposeful termination in abortion, thus leaving controversy regarding personhood aside (*Casey, 112 S. Ct. at 2859 Rehnquist, C.J.*). No one can reasonably argue that there is not human life at the moment of conception. Yet the problem is precisely that judgment as to whether the zygote is human life. Ethical judgment indeed rational judgment as we know is not always reasonable or ethical. Proponents of a woman's choice to abort will argue that for abortion to be denied it must affect the life of a living person. That approach however extends abortion beyond infancy in the womb as is evidenced in partial birth as well as actual birth. Human life

---

[31] Harry N. Scheiber, *Doctrinal Legacies and Institutional Inovations,* American Law and the Constitutional Order. Ed. by Lawrence Friedman. Cambridge, MA: Harvard University Press, 1988. p. 454.

is a process that clearly cannot be subject to arbitrary opinion about personhood. Abortion is not a right to privacy issue; it affects another life. Rehnquist's legal opinion is a valid description of personal freedom and its limitations. Justice, in this instance the right to life must be given due recognition when considering personal freedoms and the inviolability of conscience. At the end of the day there can be no exceptions to the obligation to protect the life of the innocent. No civil law can justifiably remove that right, as wrongly adjudicated in *Roe v Wade*. The case is made that we live in a pluralistic society. Pluralism means mutual tolerance. Mutual tolerance does not sanction members of the legislature especially Catholic politicians to take the position that abortion is just and that a law that permits the killing of the innocent should stand not to mention be expanded. Some Catholic politicians argue Aquinas would have sanctioned abortion based on his belief of a hiatus after conception and the development of human form. Aquinas saw creation as movement from potency to actualization. But all newly created being is a process of actualization. Person actually means entity, soul self-motivation. For man that process is sacred and begins with the transmission of human life to the undeniable specificity of human life at the moment of conception. That is why the Magisterium taught in *Humanae Vitae* that any unnatural interruption of the transmission of human life is evil. It is within Magisterial Church doctrine—not our view of a theologian's thought or what his actual intent was—that we are obliged to form our consciences. Faith is not personal opinion. Catholic politicians who have the community at large as their audience are in complicit error when they promote views that contradict Church teaching on serious matters. Free speech must be exercised with justice. Justice is the recognition of the right to life for all persons inclusive of infants in the womb and the elderly.

All human life has certain inalienable rights that are not arbitrarily subject to removal. Thus there are standards of justice intrinsic to people that constitute the dignity of man. These standards that make up natural law are the foundation of legal practice and of the protection of rights within society.

Justice in human acts consequently is required in a definition of human freedom. The recognition of just standards is precisely the recognition of teleological ends in human nature. That propensity in man toward truth fleshes-out the meaning of just standards expressed in singular principles of acts. Standards have no real efficacy without the latter. To understand the doctrine of singular principles of acts is to appreciate what man is. From them we infer what his ultimate end is and in what manner he acts toward that end. It is an observable process that defines ethics. Universal standards are specified in things we do. Unless justice is posited in human acts we are liable to injustice. Unless the relationship of natural law to civil justice is recognized then individual rights that were established and protected within the tradition of the laws of nature as common law will continue to be subject to modifications that remove those inherent rights.

As has occurred historically, when there is no adherence to inviolable standards of justice drawn from the natural law, then the rationalization and practice of euthanasia, abortion, the killing of the handicapped, of persons diagnosed as incompetent, and of those considered unworthy of life is inevitable. The eugenics oriented euthanasia promoted in pre-war Germany by legal scholar Karl Binding and psychiatrist Alfred Hoche in their classic 1920 *Authorization to End Life Unworthy of Life* was couched in appeals to humanitarian sentiment. End unnecessary suffering. Eventually, as Henry Friedlander points out in *The Origins of Nazi Genocide*, the appeal would be to rid society of so-called genetic mentally and physically defective persons who might 'infect' the population.

Friedlander, professor of history at Brooklyn College wrote a well documented account of the Holocaust. While he cites abuses by Catholics, he includes the heroism of many. He adds that the German Catholic hierarchy at the zenith of Nazi power issued an important statement on the right to life of the innocent. It sent a memorandum addressing that right to the Reich minister of church affairs; it also issued a pastoral letter, read from the pulpits of all Catholic churches on 6 July 1941, warning that "never, under any circumstances, except in war and justified self-defense, is it permissible to kill an innocent human being."[32] The opposition of the churches briefly delayed the murder of innocent people in Germany and contributed to restoring a national conscience. But homicide of 'inferior' peoples continued in Poland since 1939 and on a massive scale after the June 1941 invasion of Russia. The book documents the development of cultural attitudes that precipitated Nazi ideology and the Holocaust.

In America famed jurist Oliver Wendell Holmes Jr took to the eugenics of the early 20th century. Holmes ruled to sterilize the mentally handicapped. His purpose was to limit the number of 'morons' in America. Early 20th century eugenics colors much of the theory behind contemporary genetics. The thrust of eugenics and genetics is the improvement of humanity by eliminating the 'flawed'. The Nazi appeal to kill the handicapped and end unnecessary suffering was as said drawn from eugenics doctrines and its ideology of race cleansing. It has resurfaced in the Netherlands and in the Oregon State referendum on euthanasia. It

---

[32] Henry Friedlander. *The Origins of Nazi Genocide: From Euthanasia to the Final Solution.* Chapel Hill: The University of North Carolina Press, 1999. pp. 114-115.

is particularly evident in abortions of impaired infants meant to prevent the proliferation of genetic disorders.

There is then a moral targeting belonging to our species that finds its mark in ends that avoids killing the innocent and protects them. They are predetermined insofar as the good of ends are reflective of a divinely instituted order both as ends of nature and ends of acts. Ends of acts are not determined by men but God since the natural law in man reflects the eternal law. The unbiased free thought of moral persons discovers them. Morality requires the pursuit of truth and the moral courage to implement it. Truth challenges our complacency. Consequently morality is exercised with a commitment to truth in complete freedom.

American justice as well as international law embodies precepts derived from human nature. Furthermore the natural law and the virtuous practice of justice from which it is derived elevate human reason to the level of the divine intelligence.

> The rational creature partakes of a share of providence being provident both for itself and for others. It has a natural inclination to its proper act and end, and this participation of the eternal law in the rational creature is called the natural law (*ST Ia2ae 91, 2*).

A practical knowledge of good and evil is available through the natural light of reason reflecting upon the natural law. The sources of our complete knowledge of human nature and the teleological ends of acts as said are drawn from both revelation and reason.

Man has the natural capacity to draw the structure of moral acts from what is perceived in existence. Reason first finds that structure in the life and movement of things toward their proper ends. As noted it is not the ends of nature alone that comprises the natural law. The natural law is intelligible and completed in acts that the intellect apprehends as good. The intellect possesses the natural capacity of identifying good in human acts following deliberation of the conditions of the act. That explains why it is from knowledge of the good perceived in acts that the general principles of the natural law are inferred. Moral living is essentially a reflection of the divine good evident in human acts. Every pursuit of man is ordained toward its ultimate end in acts that are good.

If moral virtue is naturally acquired by reason, the principle source of discernment of a higher level of virtue is given through the gifts of the Holy Spirit. Apprehension of the supreme good in human acts is essentially the work of grace. Although Aristotle and Aquinas are in agreement that a fundamental level of truth in human acts, the general principles of the natural law, is available to us on a natural, acquired level, it is not always perfectly apprehended. Aquinas clarified that distinction on justice in *ST 2a2ae.*

Aquinas certainly recognized that ethics could not exclude the supernatural as the primary source of knowledge of the supreme good. That exclusion is seen in contemporary secular humanism, which rejects religious belief as a source of ethical discernment. An ethics based entirely on the rationale of the common good, which good secular humanists generally acknowledge, would nonetheless be prone to impinge on individual rights. Again the reason is ethics is grounded in perception and that reasoned knowledge of human nature from which standards of justice are inferred. General ideas however lofty do not specify what good is in factual implementation.

Moral virtue enhances our vision of what is right. It does not mean that the person who lacks virtue is blind to truth, he simply wills not to accept a higher level of moral truth. Blindness in this instance is not visual but moral. No one is devoid of virtue. Every person is capable of making ethical decisions and must make such decisions in order to fit in with society. There is a difference between the good citizen who practices virtue for expediency and the virtuous person who does so in pursuit of good for its own sake. Even the enhancement of moral perspicacity from a naturally acquired perspective has more to do with personal conviction, meaning the cultivation of a moral conscience, than it does with learning and experience. A virtuous disposition is what actually sharpens our moral vision. Therefore spiritual enlightenment cannot be entirely ruled out during the pre-Christian era. Throughout the history of ancient Greece and Rome individuals practiced high levels of moral behavior. No one can say with certitude whether some such individuals were not the recipients of grace. It can however be said unequivocally that throughout the history of ancient Israel there were persons like Judith and Moses who received spiritual favor.

If spiritual blindness is a responsible fault by disposition it does not mean that a person who does not apprehend what is right in some instances is immoral. Reason in assessing actions is not always easy. That can be attributed to the human condition. Similarly it is unreasonable to assume that someone who struggles to be virtuous and is inconsistent in practice is immoral. Humanness evidently has its limitations. Although virtue is naturally acquired by reason, reason is insufficient in discernment.

> It is necessary that there should be some perfection of man whereby he is ordered to the supernatural end which exceeds the capacity of man's natural principles. But this can only be if over and above the natural principles there are supernatural principles of action infused in man by God (*Virt Cmn 10*).

Discernment and consistent practice has its primary source in the infused gifts of the Holy Spirit. This deserves repeating here because it clarifies the parameters of conceptual knowledge. Again general knowledge of good, which men historically share, is naturally acquired and conceptual. Like all principles of knowledge that by their nature transcend material existence they are known by analogy. One first perceives good in things. Then from numerous individual examples perceived in actions we draw a wider sense of that good. The analogy is made from what is perceived as good in acts to a generalization that finds its own parameters within the concept, which is to say that as conceptual it is definable. The difficulty is what exactly is definable. If we say that to give a glass of cold water to a thirsty person, to share our food with the hungry, or to give a needy person a jacket for warmth is charity the definition finds intelligibility in individual acts. But what is the comparison of particulars to in forming our universal concept? Is it a feeling or conviction that renders substance to the concept? Feeling is generic unless specified. And if we define charity we are setting the limitations of charity. But contrary to that assumption charity is not subject to perceivable limitation. The analogy rests on the corresponding realization that the extension of charity surpasses its intellectual conceptualization. What I know intellectually in respect to good is always a generalization that while subject to being worded and thereby defined in examples is in its possible meaning limitless. It becomes obvious that the concept is merely a principle of human knowledge, and in every instance a limited knowledge, that does not necessarily contain all that the concept indicates, or suggests to me.

What then motivates us to do what is morally good when it is not desired out of expectation of outcome if not divinely inspired love? Intellectual concepts have no reality outside the mind that forms them. It is in effect an inner sense of doing the right thing. What else can we attribute to this kind of desire except a love of justice for its own sake? That opens up the query of transcendent good. What exactly is it that we target when justice is loved for its own sake? Some have argued that altruism is complimentary give and take behavior and therefore reducible to reward seeking. If it is love of an invisible God some say that one can love a poet who never existed. That does not explain the selfless love not found in any other religion that Christ's faithful have for others. This kind of selfless love has no rationale. It transcends reason. We may love another for their sake and die for them but only one object of love can elicit from us the compassion of giving oneself for others, as when one's true motivation is love itself. That desire must then have an intelligible target if it transcends any visibly attainable goal. There is in this kind of commitment a transformation of person that cannot occur simply on the basis of reward, such as inner peace, or even if it is the reward of eternal life. The person who commits by *faith* has to be willing to undergo that radical transformation for its own sake since the evidence for reward in this life is not invincible. We hope for it. Nevertheless faith that chooses the good for its own sake is a rational desire for an intelligible end that mysteriously identifies with the divinity. Somehow the soul knows but cannot explicate it. It is desire that transcends our normal understanding. It must be a gift. And it remains an act of faith in this life to commit oneself to this gift because what the soul perceives 'as in a darkened mirror' is not as clear as that which is evident to the senses. A living faith then is a totally free act of love. Love can only be given in freedom. Only in the beatific vision of God in heaven will faith be unnecessary and our knowledge of Him become perfect and made absolutely clear. The supreme human act will be our love and praise of God. Insofar as we live on this earth we may by a life of charity and contemplation reach an intimate but still imperfect knowledge of God. Nonetheless most devoted Christians attain some form of true knowledge.

The ultimate end is the Supreme Good identified by Aquinas as that to which all desire for good aims. That Supreme Good is God. God is the teleological end of all things, and for man God is the end of all desire for pleasure and happiness. It is difficult to convince someone who does not hold to this that the reason why some perceive spiritual truth where others do not is the absence of faith and that level of moral virtue that is a gift. If one's vision of truth in lesser matters is clouded as such the broader view of life will likewise be affected. Natural law from the perspective of a secularized culture inhibits freedom. What is wrongly perceived as deterministic in the laws of nature is actually the source of freedom. If we did not possess the inherent propensity toward good that enables us to apprehend it then the only alternative would be secularism. Issues like global warming and cigarettes become the only legitimate moral issues of the day.

How then does the ethicist address justice in a society that is increasingly secular and ignorant of the rights that define human nature and the practice of justice? There is nothing preventing the ethicist from examining the causes of human behavior from the perspective of the human sciences as well as the natural law. A common ground is possible because these sciences study man. In fact the behavioral sciences have much to offer if the research is both rigorous and honest. Scientists cannot close their minds to truth on any level. The logical place to start is our natural sense of what matters in respect to our own person, life and liberty and all the rights that define our human nature and are precious to us. If we recognize these just rights for ourselves then we are capable of recognizing them in others. The recognition and respect of those rights in others is the practice of justice.

Laws proceed from justice and not by necessity the converse. Justice the proper source of law is best defined as love of neighbor. We practice justice in relation to him and to act justly includes the practice of prudence, wisdom, which is akin to prudence, fortitude, temperance, compassion, humility, generosity, mercy, forgiveness, magnanimity and so forth. Therefore Aquinas rightly said justice is that single cardinal virtue that incorporates all the virtues. Later in 1370 Saint Catherine of Siena in her *Dialogue, A Treatise on Divine Providence no.19* cites the Divine Wisdom that "Every virtue and every defect is obtained by means of our neighbor." Knowledge of what is just commands us to interact accordingly. That inner persuasion is what we call conscience.

5. CONSCIENCE

Conscience is that inherent dynamic in man that encourages virtuous behavior. To possess a conscientious attitude means that we must also possess prescient knowledge of right and wrong behavior. That knowledge may be learned. The problem with learned knowledge is whether it is correct. Reason has a terminal point called apprehension. Without this full realization of the intellect in apprehension reason would remain an endless and futile process. That is precisely what occurs when arguments are made for and against some moral issue when neither party possesses, or better said does not exercise this inherent capacity of the mind to identify good and evil. If that—the inherent capacity to identify good and evil were not the case then not only would one's conscience be absolutely inviolable but anyone might make any argument regarding right and wrong and remain solvent in their position. Put another way responsibility would be an empty term. Therefore man must have an inherent capacity to identify truth that is at the very core of conscience. Based on this doctrine of an inherent capacity to identify good and evil no one can claim to be in good conscience in committing an act that by its nature, such as murder and false witness is always reprehensible and evil.

Saint Thomas Aquinas says conscience exhorts us to do what is right, reprimands when we falter, and causes remorse when we sin. It is perceived as a voice. Conscience however is first understood as an act (*ST Ia 79, 13*). Literally it means to act with knowledge. Of all the diverse inclinations in man that form conscience synderesis, the retention of the first principles of the natural law, is the primary inclination that gives it its form. Without a general knowledge of right and wrong man has no real guidance in directing his actions. This implies that in order to begin the specification of good in acts one must already possess some form of knowledge. As said these are the inborn principles of the natural law, the reflection in man of the eternal law.

False conscience and ignorance is described in *ST Ia2ae 6, 1-8* on *Voluntary and Involuntary* and viewed under three conditions. The first is concomitant, meaning an involuntary act due to ignorance that is nonetheless voluntary in respect to the will. Someone takes what he assumes is an envelope containing another's salary that actually belongs to him, the person attempting to steal. Consequent ignorance describes a voluntary act and responsibility due to something someone can and ought to know. A person pursues a relationship and commits adultery. Another example is drinking to excess and causing a fatal auto accident. Antecedent is ignorance prior to a wrongful act that someone would have avoided had they known. Antecedent ignorance is false conscience but there is no responsibility for sin. The polygamy of the Patriarchs Abraham, David, and Solomon is an example. Augustine and Aquinas believed that they were not guilty of sin because they violated a secondary principle of the natural law, monogamy, out of ignorance, and not a first principle, which is conjugal relations with women in some form of contractual agreement such as marriage as it was understood, or the possession of concubines. Augustine and Aquinas cite cultural mores and the difficulty involved in arriving at the complete truth through reason. That is not so in respect to consequent ignorance.

> Ever since the creation of the world his invisible nature, namely, his eternal power and deity, has been clearly perceived in the things that have been made. So they are without excuse; for although they knew God they did not honor him as God or give thanks to him (*Rm 1:18-22*).

Reason is ordered to its proper end and act, as said, as is the will. Not to comply is to be responsible for one's ignorance. Obviously for the Romans castigated by Paul it was serious matter. However, the Patriarchs were absolved. What about discernment and the inviolability of conscience? Paul says the Romans did know. Aquinas says the Patriarchs did not. To what extent can it be said that the Romans actually discerned the truth about God and to what extent does inviolability of conscience come into play?

The inviolability of conscience is said to require us to pursue its dictates even when false. Although Aquinas assumes conscience binds theoretically in any instance, such binding is conditional.

> One who follows such a conscience and acts according to it acts against the law of God and sins mortally. For there was sin in the error itself, since it happened because of ignorance of what one should have known. (*De Ver 17, 4 Ad 3*).

Again it is the understanding of consequent ignorance that determines guilt or innocence in respect to the weightier principles of the natural law. The doctrine on conscience as already seen in respect to responsibility assumes that the first principles of the law of nature remain binding and failure to identify them is more an elective deficit of the will than comprehension. Discernment of those principles begins with reflexive knowledge of the natural inclinations to some good and the process by which conscience is formed.

As regards conflicts of conscience there is insufficient communication of the need to assent to the moral teachings of the Roman Pontiff, specifically those not solemnly defined but known by their tone, nature, and frequent repetition—such as teaching on contraception—as contained in *Lumen Gentium n. 25* 1964 and reaffirmed as the third level of adherence to truth in the *Doctrinal*

Commentary n. 12 1998 on the apostolic letter *Ad Tuendam Fidem* 1998 of John Paul II. Unfortunately the Vatican II 1965 *Declaration on Religious Freedom* was widely considered recognition of the right to conscientiously disregard the ban on contraception.

> The inquiry [on truth] is to be free. Man acknowledges the imperatives of the divine law through the mediation of conscience. Man is not to be restrained from acting in accordance with his conscience (*excerpts from article 3*).

At that time Cardinal Cushing withdrew opposition to a Massachusetts legislative effort to strike down state law prohibiting sale and information of contraceptives to unmarried persons. His stated intention was to not impose Catholic teaching on non Catholics. The *Declaration* addresses those seeking the truth not Catholics who have made their profession of faith to the truth. Nevertheless many lay persons and non Catholic commentators unfamiliar with Church teaching came to the opposite conclusion. There were also contrapositions to Church teaching on contraception by Catholic authors, professors, and even clergy since 1963. For large numbers of Catholics contraception became a matter of conscience. In 1968 Paul VI responded with *Humanae Vitae* and declared its use serious sin because it is contrary to human love and the transmission of life. Opposition continued. Many laity understandably still considers contraception a conscience issue. This can be corrected by common effort. Though the causes for widespread breakdowns of morality and marriage since 1963 are thought to be multiple lack of adherence to doctrine is the major factor. Man needs sound witness to truth to practice the faith. That witness is the task of all Christians.

Man is naturally inclined toward good. But again the perfection of man's natural inclinations by grace, infused virtue exceeds his nature (*ST Ia2ae 51, 4 c*). Thus the natural virtues and dispositions are strengthened by infused virtue (*ST Ia2ae 51, 4 Ad 3*). Basically good but weak persons become faithful and holy persons.

While those virtues and inclinations natural to man are spiritually strengthened to exceed man's natural capacity, human nature does not undergo essential change. What undergoes change in becoming good is man's perfection. If grace does not change our human nature then neither does sin. This refers to sin whether original or elective. Although original sin is applicable to all since the fall of Adam and Eve it is a penalty in the form of an estrangement from God rather than change in human nature. God does not re-create man through grace. He is bringing human nature to perfection by restoring what was actually lost through original sin. Sin consequently is not brought about by a change in human nature, as if that were a change that could be considered natural. It is always a free deviation of the will. The importance of this from an anthropological perspective is twofold. Human nature as said is not subject to change. The other important point is that there already exists in man the dynamic toward perfection. Insofar as perfection is not actualized that dynamic is there as potency. As regards original sin Augustine, Aquinas, and others thought it warranted condemnation. In 1201 Pope Innocent III in a letter to the Archbishop of Arles instructed only those who commit serious sin and refuse to repent are subject to condemnation, not those who are not baptized and thereby withheld the Beatific Vision. Thus we had in the Church the opinion of an after death indeterminate state called Limbo for the non-baptized infant. At present the Church endorses the assumption stated in *The Catholic Catechism no. 1261* that non-baptized who do not commit serious sin but are withheld the vision of God are subject to God's mercy. The Spanish theologians struggled with this question after the discovery of the New World. They came to the view that salvation since the crucifixion and resurrection of Christ is available to all men through their willingness to accept grace, notwithstanding its difficulty without baptism and the Gospels. Christ did say that there are many rooms in his Father's mansion. There are good people who were never baptized whether living in a western metropolis or the rain forests of the Amazon. Here theologians speak of a baptism of desire. What that may mean is frequently difficult to say. But it is understood in the conscientious act of philosopher Henri Bergson, a French Jew who asked that a priest be present at his burial. That understanding differs when considering non baptized infants. That infant nonetheless may respond in a way that only God recognizes. We must also give account to the non baptized Abraham, Moses, Judith, Elijah, the Holy Innocents, et Al. who we may assume enjoy the Beatific Vision. Baptism ensures availability of salvation and eternal happiness. Grace is seen to suffice in ways suited to individual instances where baptism is not available.

All men then have the natural capacity to distinguish between good and evil. Otherwise as said there would be no moral responsibility for those who rationalize and argue for the legitimacy of immoral acts. Conscience would be made irrelevant. It is clear that homosexual acts with children, or the promotion of homosexuality should not be tolerated by civil law, or by society at large. The assumption that it is okay to be a practicing gay is a form of promotion and has nothing to do with being compassionate, or for that matter, tolerant. Befriending a homosexual can be both tolerant and compassionate, but cannot be made equivalent to moral approval. Homosexuality is not human love. Human love has an ordered purpose. For example Paul VI said human love is the primary reason why the faithful should reject contraceptives in *Humanae Vitae* and that conjugal love is total giving of the self to the other. It is giving of oneself that by its nature is love for human life. He was convinced that human love is minimized when there is intervention to omit the transmission of life from the act. The conjugal act, which is meant to increase the spiritual dimension of love, is narrowed. As said in spite of the publication of *Humanae Vitae* contraception became widely accepted within and outside the Catholic Church. Corresponding to this acceptance there has been not simply a continued relaxation of sexual mores, but the increase of perverted sexual practices, the erosion of marriage, the association of sex with the grotesque, with violence, the devaluation of women, and with death. We should consider if this is mere coincidence.

Unfortunately as I have learned from hearing confessions the conscience of many penitents is not informed on Church teaching regarding sexual behavior and the transmission of human life. Those of us who represent doctrinal authority by ordination have the serious obligation to inform the faithful as to what is sinful. As regards the laity appointed by that authority to offer religious instruction it also has the obligation to teach, in season and out of season what is morally reprehensible and serious. Insofar as laity not so assigned they also cannot misrepresent Church doctrine and disseminate falsehoods. Although it is clear that the far greater responsibility lies with those of us who are ordained. The attitude of many is to remain silent on these issues due to what they consider the inviolable area of conscience. Nevertheless the responsibility of all persons regarding serious matter whether Catholic or not cannot be dismissed on the basis of lack of knowledge. We have already seen that there are things we should know by inquiry and education. Furthermore conscience cannot be viewed inviolable even when the consensus of a culture holds that certain acts are morally correct. We remind ourselves of Germany's Hitler Youth. Here we have the question whether someone indoctrinated from childhood that murdering Jews is a good thing is responsible when committing those murders. Those who disseminate and those who practice remain responsible since it is an interior decision that denies the dictates of the voice of the soul. No pretension of religious practice or rationale in any circumstances can condone the murder of innocent people. The first principle of the natural law is binding whenever it refers to serious matter like murder, false witness, pedophilia, and adultery. Such sins are evident to us by our very nature as persons created in God's image. It cannot be argued that ignorance of God and the commandments absolved mankind from sin. If that were so there would be no need for the Crucified Christ. Jew as well as gentile was subject to divine justice. Again man possesses the inherent capacity to discern the Supreme Good.

Cornelio Fabro discussed the question of atheism and salvation in *God in Exile*: *Modern Atheism.* The celebrated priest philosopher-theologian believed that all non believers during their lifetime arrive at a given threshold of knowledge of truth requiring them to make a conscientious choice either to accept the existence of God or not. That obligation of conscience was as seen held by St Paul in his letter *Romans 1, 18-32.* He perceived condemnation for those, here not the Jews who possessed the prophets and the commandments but rather the gentile Romans who should have known God through recognition of his divinity in the order of nature. On that note Catholicism does not deny evolution. Rather it insists that reason proves the existence of a First Principle. Whether man evolved from a lower species it remains certain that man's unique capacity to reason could not have spontaneously emerged from the physical world. Faith then is a willingness to believe what reason and conscience tell us is true. Finally Sweden's Dag Hammarskjöld former UN secretary was thought an atheist and did much to advance integrity and justice. We know a tree by its fruit. God alone knows a man's heart.

There is an issue of degrees of belief for those of us who have made formal acceptance of a faith like Catholicism. Conscience is at the heart of that issue because in today's Church many are selective in their adherence to moral as well as theological doctrine. For American Catholics—as well as Catholics elsewhere the efficacy of magisterial teaching is in question, whether it is on abortion, sterilization, euthanasia, contraception, and social justice. There are several encyclicals on the morality of economic policy, government programs, and finance. For instances, consolidating power and acquiring wealth is unethical if detrimental to the just needs of others. As stewards of creation we are obliged to provide reasonable protection of the environment.

There are truths that are not clear and which require study and evaluation, as well as that which is actually evil but may present itself to us under the guise of truth. Lack of clarity on Church doctrine among Catholics and the spread of error is obviously a problem. A Catholic author publicly stated that many young Catholics commit abortion not knowing it is sinful and are therefore invincibly ignorant and free of sin. Again we cannot be invincibly ignorant of acts that violate the first principles of the natural law because we know them by nature, acts such as murder, false witness, pedophilia, adultery, and the killing of innocents. Invincible ignorance refers to knowledge beyond a person's capacity to know (*ST Ia2ae 76, 2*). Abortion makes that unlikely. Pope Pius IX confirms this in his encyclical *Singulari Quidem A. 7* excusing ignorance beyond someone's control. As noted regarding consequent ignorance if a person were unaware of serious matter like abortion they are still bound to know and are responsible (*ST Ia2ae 76, 2 Ad 5*). Nevertheless there are extenuating circumstances for some such as intellectual impairment, anxiety due to impoverished circumstances, fear of reprisal, and similar severe circumstances which are frequently coupled with a kind of innocent uneducated ignorance that inhibit a truly free choice and lessen culpability.

False conscience for the most part and the consequent devaluing of the Eucharist are at the heart of the current spread of apostasy. The spread of falsehood is wide and the need to be informed and discern what is presented to us is vital.

6. DISCERNMENT OF SPIRITS

There are many things that touch our lives and shape our thoughts in this world. They range from a friend's opinion on moral issues to political ideologies. While some of that which is communicated to us can be considered negligible much else deserves scrutiny. The reason is that there are two real spirits that influence what the world says and does. The first is the Holy Spirit. The other is the spirit of the Satanic. The Holy Spirit is first because of God's preeminence. That does not mean the Holy Spirit possesses the greater influence in world affairs. To the contrary attitudes that are presently shaping human rights, social justice, and sexual morality appear increasingly in conflict to what Christianity understands as good. Evil has often been dismissed as a passé term but lately has come to be more closely scrutinized. It is filled with complex meaning. For example what comes under the cloak of educational freedom often seems evil. Is it educational freedom when government controlled education permits just one evolutionary theory to be taught, that precludes the existence of God and prohibits alternatives like intelligent design? Is mandating our children be taught immoral practices are okay educational freedom? Discrimination is a legal term that refers to classes of people distinguished by ethnicity, religion, and social status. But deviate behavior does not constitute a class of people. Politicians and the legal system defend a presumed right of any person access to any social institution. Keeping the balance between democracy and freedom of religion in America demands legislators protect the interests of both. That balance is shifted when government imposes laws that unjustly deny religious freedom. Aquinas said the law is a plan for justice. Good plans do not always work. That is mostly due to those who implement them.

The bogus description of discrimination by the courts and prejudicial government education policy both point to the atheistic and radical egalitarian secularization of society. A godless level playing field is the aim of politicians that misrepresent the First Amendment which prohibits establishment by government of a religion as was instituted in England. Far from confirming atheistic secularization the American Constitution intended to protect freedom of religion. This kind of secularization is abandonment of belief in God. It inhibits the practice of moral behavior that stems from religious tradition. The trend toward complete secularization of government by legislation that attacks life is apparent in *Roe v Wade.* It reflects what is transpiring within our culture. But it is frequently the case that government itself sets the tone for an egalitarian godless society evident in mandating universal access to partial birth abortion, federal artificial birth control programs, sterilization, funding of abortion clinics, and federal interference in military policy on gays. The more the government creates and imposes such policies the greater the apparent willingness among people to accept them. People can be led to believe that these immoral positions constitute democratic reform. Government is instead replacing religion with its own moral views. The responsibility lies with our leaders as well as with the public to elect persons in the executive and legislative branches of government who have moral conviction and who will lead accordingly. The judicial branch is filled by executive appointment. Nonetheless the legislative branch must confirm or reject and it is here where those elected to congress, particularly Catholics have an obligation to confirm jurists who hold to sound moral values as well as judicial acumen. No institution however enlightened can remove the right to life of the innocent. Liberals have more voice in defending their positions by imposing a litmus test on jurists selected for appointment to the Supreme Court whereas Christians and others who hold to traditional values are impugned as theocrats opposed to the Constitution.

At times evil can slip undetected under the law and find protection. An example is when the Apostle Paul and his companion Silas were in Philippi; a Latin speaking colony under Roman law in Greece largely populated by veterans of the Roman army. It was here that the event that led to his imprisonment and miraculous escape occurred.

> A slave-girl who was a soothsayer made a lot of money for her masters by foretelling the future. This girl started following Paul and the rest of us shouting, 'Here are the servants of the Most High God; they have come to tell you how to be saved!' She did this day after day until Paul was exasperated and turned around and said to the spirit, 'I order you in the name of Jesus Christ to leave that woman.' The spirit went out of her then and there (*Ac 16, 16-18*).

Paul tolerated her for several days before his rebuke. On the surface there seems to have been nothing wrong with the girl's heralding Paul. She spoke the truth about his mission. Paul's tolerance implies acceptance of that. Why did Paul finally take exception to her proclaiming his mission? The clue to Paul's admonition and what enfolds is that she was according to the English text a soothsayer. But the original Greek text says something more foreboding. She was possessed by a Python-spirit, a reference to the serpent Python of the Delphic oracle, which indicates the Satanic.

Paul's anger was probably similar to Christ's admonishment of the demonic spirits to be silent when they heralded him. Heralding someone can have evil purpose. Overstating someone's importance carries with it the nuance of sarcasm and disposes the onlooker to suspicion. Furthermore it presents the religious messenger forcefully in the manner of one who is proselytizing. Later the girl's masters had Paul and Silas arrested, beaten, and imprisoned on the false charge that they were proselytizing, which was against Roman law. That Paul unlike the Roman authorities was able to see through the girl's 'witness' speaks to the charism he describes as the gift of discerning spirits in *1 Cor 12, 10.* Aquinas acknowledges Paul's teaching that discernment of spirits is a gift of the Holy Spirit (*ST 2a2ae 171, Art 1*). He goes on to say that some prophesy is from God and some from the heart of the prophet indicating that the latter is not always precise. An example of the latter is a prophet's prediction of an event the time of which God may extend. We see this in the Apostles' assumption that the final days were at hand in their anticipation of apocalyptic calamity, which turned out to be the Roman destruction of the Jewish nation in 70 A.D. Also, Aquinas says demons because of their greater knowledge of things are able to make predictions of events that the lesser intellect of man has difficulty foreseeing. Such would explain the demonic witnesses to Christ in the Gospels. At the same time demons cannot know the mind of God and true prophesy. Therefore their witness to Christ is not based on faith [a gift] but on knowledge of scripture and indication of events. Solely in consideration of the plethora of articles and books about the identity of Christ, much of which is false the significance of the Holy Spirit's gift of discernment is immense. Anyone who sincerely turns to Christ would be given some measure of that ability. It is reasonable to assume that this charism is especially given to bishops and most specifically the Roman Pontiff.

The need for spiritual discernment extends beyond literature. It includes all forms of media associated with two cultural phenomena, New Age and Secular Humanism. New Age is an amorphous trend within modern society toward self-apotheosis. As such it is not specific to any one movement but encompasses that basic ideology found in modern day Gnosticism and Secular Humanism. But the overall appeal is couched in spirituality albeit different from that of traditional religion. That is where the danger for many lies: "It is not every spirit, my dear people that you can trust. Test them, to see if they come from God" (*1 Jn 4, 1*). New Age encompasses the rebirth of Gnosticism, pseudo theologies that focus on self-revelation and with secular movements in academia and politics that share the common belief that the person is the ultimate measure of truth.

SECULAR HUMANISM

Secular Humanism differs in that it repudiates belief in God but offers a new form of piety, albeit without religious belief. For the many trending toward agnosticism it offers an attractive alternative to religion. Dr. Paul Kurtz, a professor of philosophy has served as president of the Council on Secular Humanism. Dr. Kurtz has enlisted an impressive group of philosophers, academics, ethicists who by disposition repudiate Aquinas' approach to truth.[33] The Council's 1973 *Humanist Manifesto II* is a call for freedom from belief in God and the cleansing of ethics from all irrational belief, the presumption being that all religious belief is irrational. Genuine spiritual experience Dr. Kurtz says does not involve belief in the soul and any other spiritual existence. As such it reflects the

[33] Signatories include Albert Ellis, Sidney Hook, Joseph Fletcher, W.V. Quine, Sir A.J. Ayer, Kai Nielsen, Sir Raymond Firth, B.J. Skinner.

nihilist thought of the death of God theologies. *A Secular Humanist Declaration* published 1980 argues that religious belief inhibits free thought and the development of ethical standards. In his *Declaration* Dr. Kurtz cites as models for reasoned inquiry Lucretius, Epicurus, David Hume, and Bertrand Russell all of whom reject rational inference from the physical world and belief in transcendent truth.

Secular Humanism's *Declaration* cites principles of tolerance, compromise, and the negotiation of differences. At first it seems to suggest a new inclusive doctrine. But the *Declaration* continues its renunciation of the spiritual soul and in a god who created man in his image. Kurtz's *Declaration* warns against the "reappearance" of "authoritarian religions" and "the reassertion of orthodox authority by the Roman Catholic papal hierarchy" (*Declaration, Introduction*). Accusing today's Church of moral imposition is commonplace but not as pronounced as by secular humanists (see *Declaration, 4. Ethics Based On Critical Intelligence*). What this does is establish that the "one church" they falsely accuse of imposition on the whole of society, the Catholic Church stands as the institution that in its official teaching capacity remains consistent and clearly viable, and consequently poses the greatest challenge to their errors. Appeal to the complete truth obviously does not find favor among secularists. Nevertheless Kurtz recognizes the good that Christianity has accomplished through the centuries, the building of hospitals and schools, the encouragement "of the spirit of love and charity". Kurtz's admiration of the good the Church has accomplished coupled with his repudiation of its moral authority indicates not only his unwillingness to appreciate the life style that promotes moral virtue but his issue with the exclusivity of truth. But as such it still shows some honesty. The rejection of truth as seen is not entirely a matter of comprehension. Assent to truth also requires consent to the gift of grace. Grace is always available as is hope for changes of attitude. Therefore for Christians the inclusion of prayer rather than counter arguments alone is the better approach to secularism.

New Age does not share the atheism of secular humanism. Claiming enlightened intellectual superiority to institutional religion it has much in common with the Gnosticism of early Christianity and 'progressive' thought within today's Christianity.

NEO -GNOSTICISM

Author and professor of religion Elaine Pagels, in her touching and beautifully written opening to *Beyond Belief* invites the reader to share her anguish over the terminal condition of her young son, and the re-awakening in her of religious sentiment. Pagels had previously rejected conventional religion and its emphasis on doctrine. She felt it did not address the need for spiritual transformation. The book's theme begins with her learning of her son's deadly illness and the chance encounter with the congregation of a Manhattan church. The small group is open to diverse views and focused on community support. Healing is found in personal encounter, admitting to feelings of despair and dealing with them openly, and then regaining strength in self-reliance. The anecdote supports the book's dual message. The first is that religion that promotes self-discovery has value. The second is similar but radical. It is the Gnostic position that the Church's Kerygma, which is its authoritative teaching about Christ is not really about Christ. Gnostics instead believe that Christ called us to discern the truth within ourselves. That positions the claim that He is the Truth in a very different context than that of the Church. That sets the tone for a partly exegetical, but mainly interpretive historical defense of this fundamental Gnostic position. Gnostics claim it is found in other gospels, notably the *Thomas Gospel* that is not accepted by traditional Christian churches.

The popularity of Elaine Pagels' books on Gnostic teaching in *The Gnostic Gospels* and *Beyond Belief* reflects the trend in society toward authenticity found in self-realization. Discernment from the Gnostic perspective is introspective. The discovery of one's inner self is the hallmark of truth. Gnostics also attempt to draw validation from texts in the canonical gospels that they presume agree with their teaching. The Gospel of John however was singled out for its incompatibility with their concept of mystery and doctrine of self-revelation.

Saint Irenaeus Bishop of Lyon c. 180 A.D. stands out as Gnosticism's most salient opponent and repudiated the Gnostic interpretation of John and other canonical texts. Pagels makes the provocative rhetorical argument that it is not John's central theme of the divinity of Christ, that He is the true light that is in question. John she says is clearly in accord with the established Church. How John's gospel was chosen to represent the truth is at issue. Pagels credits that to a diversity of events, which are the concerted opposition to Gnosticism, which includes the Apostle John and the Gospel attributed to him, and Saint Irenaeus and his efforts to "construct the basic architecture" of orthodox Christianity.[34] As Christianity spread two diverse forms of Christian belief developed. One is Gnosticism, which grew alongside the other increasingly organized canonical church. Spokesmen for Gnosticism Valentinus and Marcion were successful in spreading their credo. But Gnostics remained aloof and decentralized. The causes were the Gnostic beliefs in

---

[34] Elaine Pagels. *Beyond Belief. The Secret Gospel of Thomas.* New York: Random House, 2003. p. 142.

individual freedom and their assumed possession of superior knowledge. If truth is found within oneself then who needs external authority? Emperor Constantine's conversion to Christianity 312 AD added a new dimension. Pagels alleges Constantine embraced the canonical church with its hierarchy commending responsibility to Roman authority to consolidate Roman power. Actually the Edict of Milan 313 AD mandated tolerance for all religion. Constantine's invocation of the Council of Nicaea 325 AD however confirmed the more traditional witness to Christ as opposed to the Gnostic leaning Arius who denied the humanity of Christ. Constantine later suppressed Roman idolatry not Gnosticism. Still the historical argument has merit if the Church were simply a human institution. Similarly the argument is viable considering the human condition and the likely intervention of divine providence in establishing the Church.

Pagels thesis in defense of Gnostic belief compares the *Didache* to the secretive Thomas gospel. She assumes since the *Didache* was written before the canonical gospels it fits into the large category of what are called secretive writings that include the Gnostic texts. Her attention to secrets corresponds to the Gnostic sense of mystique and is seen in the Gnostic version of Peter's profession of faith. What unfolds is a revelation of such secretive meanings reserved only for the Apostle Thomas.

In the Gnostic version the Apostle Thomas gives another form of profession of faith in which he apparently humbly declares his incapacity to define Christ and in which Christ instead confirms his authentic faith as compared to the limited understanding of Saint Peter. [35] Then Thomas is alleged to have warned the other Apostles that if he dared reveal the secrets revealed to him they would stone him. Pagels suggests since Jesus has already

---

[35] Pagels. *Beyond Belief.* p. 47.

intimated to Thomas he is his equal, since he has "drunk from the same stream" of self-knowledge that Thomas has now discovered not only has he achieved sage status but he like Christ is a god. This fits in perfectly with New Age and similar movements that perceive faith as self revelation and awareness of the divinity of self. This divinity is not at all comparable to references in the Canonical Gospels to our being gods or like gods but rather as co-equals to God. That view makes for the compounding of erroneous beliefs, in particular the commonplace error that each presumed enlightened individual not only has his own sphere of divine authority but like God determines what is ethical and what is not. It is a reversion to pride and the sin of Eve.

Gnosticism seeks to destroy belief in Christ. He becomes a signpost to the self. Quoting from Pagels on the apocryphal *Book of Thomas the Contender* Jesus tells Thomas "Since you are my twin and my true companion, examine yourself and learn who you are."[36] This is not discernment of the natural law within. Knowledge of natural law corresponds with our comprehension of the order of knowledge and of the nature of the external world. As a reflection of the eternal law it indicates in the order of nature a transcendent objective order. We perceive in the good of that order the supreme good in respect to our actions and our ultimate end in God. That order transcends the self and is perceived to be external to the self. Moreover Christ's teachings transcend the law in man and any inherent truth within. Human nature does not encompass divine truth. The Old Testament, all four gospels and the witness of the Apostles affirm that.

Jesus allegedly continues to enlighten Thomas in the same text from the *Book of Thomas the Contender* with "For whoever has not known himself knows nothing, but whoever has known himself

---

[36] Pagels. *Beyond Belief.* p. 57.

has simultaneously come to know the depth of all things."[37] To support her thesis Pagels considers the possibility of animosity between John and the doubtful Thomas. John wants to quell the growing popularity of the "Doubter."[38] Still Thomas' words after touching the physical wounds of Christ, "My Lord and my God" do not support the Gnostic claim that Thomas realized his parity with Christ. What else would Thomas not believe unless he touched the wounds except Christ's unique role as Savior God? The Resurrection was that evidence. *The Book of Thomas the Contender* omits this passage. Pagels therefore opines that John or his proxy inserted that phrase into the Gospel of John to discredit Gnostic doctrine. Pagels' thesis on John's Gospel conflicts with facts. This truth within oneself doctrine that repudiates Christ as unique Savior falls entirely out of sink with the prophetic witness of the Old Testament and the Apostolic witness of the New. The Gnostic claim to authenticity rests on the fantastic proposal that only one Apostle Thomas possessed the truth and that the remaining Apostles were in unwitting error and must have conspired with John to suppress him. Pagels' suggestion that Emperor Constantine espoused the hierarchical church as the Empire's religion and for political reasons is questionable since there is no clear record. But as alluded to political motivation on that score remains plausible because the church exists within the world of human affairs. Some of her theories are not outside the realm of possibility. The suggestion about infighting between John and Thomas is plausible. The conspiracy theory is not plausible. The suggestion that Jesus is really a signpost to knowledge of one's inner self is not at all possible.

---

[37] Pagels. *Beyond Belief.* p. 57.
[38] Pagels. *Beyond Belief.* p. 58.

What is unfortunate is that there are Catholics and others who consider Pagels' books intriguing. The major issue with Gnosticism is the direction of discernment. In the main it is movement away from the very source of truth and repudiation of evident facts. It is distancing from Christ. That of itself is antichrist by definition of the Apostles and Fathers of the Church, of the latter preeminently Saint Irenaeus. Pagels and the Gnostics selective, apocryphal exegetical argument do not follow. The evidence is that the canonical Gospels were written during the lifetime of the Apostles, were mutually confirmed by them and the Christian community and are contiguous with the God of the Old Testament. The Gnostic teachings are not. What matters in the end is the plausibility of Pagels historiography and exegesis in her interpretation of Sacred Scripture. Imagination and conjecture cannot replace science however intriguing. That appears why Pagels seeks support for her thesis in the writings of Thomas Keating, a former abbot, in author Thomas Merton, and astonishingly in Saint John of The Cross and Saint Teresa of Avila. Anyone who has studied the two Spanish mystics is well aware of their fidelity to Church teaching and their unalloyed faith in Christ as personification of truth and unique entrance to contemplative knowledge of God.

BUDDHISM

Thomas Merton's later writings showed marked interest in the methods and ends of Buddhist contemplation and arguably but wrongly offer support to her thesis. That interest has occurred in Catholicism for good reasons and for bad. Interest in knowledge is always valid. However the willingness during recent years to adopt the Buddhist cultivation of interior states of de-personalization and subsequent tranquility had a very negative impact on Christian contemplation. Inner peace is not found in detachment for its own sake. It is discovered in God's personal love, which motivates us to express that love outwardly as taught by Christ. Her mention of Thomas Keating and centering prayer as an example of Buddhist contemplation is incongruous because Keating's method is intended to bring us closer to Christ, whereas Buddhism and Gnosticism draws us away from him. Catholic contemplation finds God in and through Christ. Buddhism finds deity in an amorphous pantheism. Contemplation in the Catholic tradition does not empower or guarantee a nirvana kind of continuous emotional peace but is truly evident in the selfless charity of the contemplative. The saints never lose their unique humanness and are frequently shown to have suffered doubt and emotional as well as physical pain. Suffering has irreplaceable meaning as revealed in the Cross. Religion has taken a turn to the idea of truth within oneself that finds much of its inspiration in the practice of religion minus the discomfort of commitment to the teachings of Christ. It is reminiscent of Flannery O'Connor's short story *Wise Blood* and the Christian preacher who founds the "Church without Christ."

There is an affinity between Buddhism and Gnosticism in the focus on discovering enlightenment within as the source of well being. Buddhism has gained popularity worldwide because it does offer a philosophy of inner tranquility as religion. And there is that which is commendable about some of its teachings. The difference is that Catholicism reveals to the world a personal deity, personified in the crucified Christ who is to be loved with total commitment. Any attempt to compare the teachings of Buddhism and Gnosticism to the rich tradition of Catholic contemplation exemplified in the lives and writings of great saints among whom is John of the Cross, Teresa of Avila, and Catherine of Siena falls flat.

POWER

Spiritual discernment is a virtue that is also referenced in works of fiction. The desire for power and self-aggrandizement seem universal. Tolkien's *The Lord of the Rings* is a literary masterwork for several reasons; the most important of which is a moral message related to pride and lust for power. The book places the temptation for independence and power, which we have seen is a major moral problem, in a literary context that draws us into the discussion, "If a mortal being—a human or a hobbit, for example—possesses a Ring of Power, would he choose a moral life?"[39] The philosophical question of man's temptation for unlimited power, which is to be like God, is not originally Tolkien's but Plato's. He addressed the theme of the corruptibility of unlimited power in the *Republic* and the tale of Gyges, who discovers a magic ring. What Tolkien does differently is that he shows us "by thought and actions of living characters—why we should be moral beings, why we should live a virtuous life."[40] The "Ring" is the source of immense power that is also known to corrupt the bearer.

Plato's parallel story line that power corrupts tells the story of the shepherd Gyges who finds a magical ring that makes him invisible, uses it to seduce the king's wife, kills the king, and then become king himself. Plato follows up with dialectic argument between Socrates in defense of the moral life, and Adimantus and Glaucon who reason in favor of absolute power. Authors who have something to say are well read and aware of significant arguments made by others preceding them. Tolkien is no exception. The

---

[39] Eric Katz. *The Rings of Tolkien and Plato: Lessons in Power, Choice, and Morality*, The Lord of the Rings. p. 5.
[40] Katz. *The Rings.* p. 9.

benefit to the reader is as in the case of *The Lord of the Rings* not simply adventure but a well thought out underlying ethical narrative.

Author and Tolkien commentator Eric Katz asks the central moral questions that if we were given the choice of unlimited power, would we choose it, and if given unlimited power would we have any reason to be concerned with morality since pleasure and self-gratification would be its own reward without any fear of retribution? [41] The argument in favor of unlimited power is the best possible world in which one does whatever they wish without fear of punishment. The worst possible scenario is that in which the powerless are abused by the powerful. A compromise is tentatively reached that would avoid that abuse. Nevertheless the antagonists conclude that if unlimited power were possible we would not be moral. Plato counters that a life of immorality brings mental anguish, loss of friends, and general unhappiness. Plato, Aristotle, and consequently Aquinas distinguish the important ethical difference between pleasure and happiness. Tolkien explores another important question not raised by Plato: whether one may choose unlimited power for altruistic ends. Tolkien's response is no. From the standpoint of Aquinas this kind of absolute power corrupts man since he does not possess the proportionate nature to wield it. That is reserved to the divinity. The only option is to reject the temptation of absolute power. That is the option chosen by Middle-earth's Lords of Good Galadriel and Gandalf. Both are sorely tempted to seize the ring's power for good ends but envision the personal evil that would transpire. Is then the choice of absolute power immoral? The answer in their case is yes. That is the moral of the story. But the issue raised by Lord Acton is that all power tends to corrupt and absolute power

[41] Katz. *The Rings.* P. 7.

corrupts absolutely. Is that always true? There are two maxims here and the latter for man as said is true insofar as power that parallel's the divinity. However Englishman Lord Acton is likely referring to royal power. Royal power is not absolutely corrupting. Saints Edward the Confessor of England, Louis of France, and Stephen of Hungary attest to that. The first however refers to the tendency to corrupt. But if that tendency were an inevitable truth as suggested by the second maxim then it would seem that no one in authority would be exempt from falling into corruption. Thus the statement on face value is false if we assume that power must corrupt. Authoritative power we know is necessary within an ordered society, inclusive of the Church as well as familial structure. Aquinas addresses this issue in (*ST Ia2ae 105, Art 2 Ad 2*). He says that kingship is the best form of government while acknowledging the tendency for that power to corrupt since "it easily degenerates into tyranny." However that tendency though strong is not inevitable—if sovereign power be given to a very virtuous man. Then he adds with a nuance of humor that there are very few perfectly virtuous men. That leads us to believe if we agree with Aquinas that Lord Acton was not far from the truth.

THE FALL

The temptation in the Garden of Eden leads us to the same conclusion. The problem of evil is ultimately in relation to power, to usurp what belongs to God. For Adam and Eve the freedom to choose good instead of evil was foremost in respect to obedience to God. Obedience to the divinity in humble recognition of ones limitations is the red line that divides good and evil. The choice to disobey God is reducible to the choice to become the sole arbiter of truth and to be God's equal.

> You may eat indeed of all the trees in the garden. Nevertheless of the tree of the knowledge of good and evil you are not to eat, for on the day you eat of it you shall most surely die. (*Gen 2, 16-17*).

The Temptation for Eve was Satan's lie that God wished to withhold divinity from her and Adam. Disobey "and you will be like gods, knowing good from evil" (*Gen 3, 5*). Eve chose to disobey in order to be a god, to have unlimited power and freedom. The desire to set oneself as the arbiter of truth and values, which is to separate oneself from the divinity is also the sin of Adam and Eve. We know that to turn away from God is to turn away from the source of good. He defines good by nature of his existence. Although the good of our being remains when we embrace serious sin, and, at least in this life our physical beauty, our moral good vanishes. Except for grace we are lost.

The desire for unlimited power is the sin of Lucifer, who Judaic tradition and scripture tells us sought to be like God. What was the most resplendent of God's creation, an intellect closest to the divine intelligence, gifted with knowledge, power, and virtue became enamored with himself. The desire for absolute power is love of self in its most perverse form. Unlimited power for created beings, which are not the source of good, can only end in being used to dominate others for ones exaltation and pleasure. Even if it were possible to dominate the minds of others to believe that pleasing such an authority were commendable and pleasurable, the satisfaction of those dominated would be perverse as history shows with Nazism. Affliction is the only possible outcome. A being with such virtual power is as in the case of Lucifer and Hitler likened to a loathsome creature that feeds itself on humanity. Satanic love of self is the utmost misery because there is nothing perceived within except utterly ugly self-consuming love. Self-love is akin to that everlasting worm that gnaws within the soul.

> God help thee, old man, thy thoughts have created a creature in thee; and he whose intense thinking thus makes him a Prometheus; a vulture feeds upon that heart forever; that vulture the very creature he creates. (Herman Melville. *Moby Dick XLIV*).

Authors have long struggled with the problem of good and evil. Herman Melville stands out prominently in American literature with his classic *Moby Dick.* Above he describes Ahab awakened from sleep by the horror of his own evil. We speak of hatred and evil as self-consuming, and indeed it is. Evil is certainly not a thing; as seen it has no formal cause. It is strictly incidental to the human will. It is literally our own creation.

The movements toward secular humanism and New Age seem disparate. The former advocate reason as it is perceived within its particular philosophy of freedom and disdains what it calls the irrational. The latter embraces all forms of belief that advances psychic power and deification of self. What both have in common are a fierce insistence on self-knowledge and independence from external truth and authority, namely from God and traditional religious values. The two, except for the difference between psychic power and rationalism, are really not that far apart. Discernment of good and evil for both is measured by the degree of personal freedom as opposed to what are considered unwarranted external prohibitions. The objective character of truth and knowledge of good and evil is virtually non existent. The desire to set up our own value systems independent of church and tradition is a manifestation of the desire for power. Catholics who pick and choose what Church doctrine to believe fall into that category. The myth is the intelligent individual uses his own judgment and does not follow the herd. Desire for personal power is also the driving force for the unreasonable increase of incomes and possessions, and escalation of position irrespective of competency or justification.

The dynamic of power in human relations is vast and has been voluminously addressed. What interests us here is its affect on the individual, particularly when there is no commensurate relation between the wielder and the degree of power. That lack is often evident not so much in the position one holds but rather in the manner in which the capacity to exert influence is wielded. Management positions on any level are frequently misused in the predatory abuse of personnel. Needless to say the power to command, how it is wielded defines who we are.

Christ said we know the tree by its fruits. That has to be considered the perceivable standard. It also applies to doctrine. If anyone says that Jesus is not the Messiah he is an anathema. Those strong words spoken by the Church Fathers have not lost their salt in the 21st century. There is a disposition in the Church today to dismiss the doctrines of original sin, the sacrament of penance, and judgment. Replacing them is the growing interest in magic, astrology, and spiritualism. The latter is not spirituality but interest in the paranormal and contact with the dead. The dead assure us there is no punishment for sins and all is well on the other side. Although the Harry Potter stories pit good against evil they are questionable for children because they espouse witchcraft in modern setting with appeal to emulate. Family theatre in Britain and America seems obsessed with tales of darkness. Fantasy is a form of art. Nevertheless interest in the paranormal and witchcraft is more than literary diversion when it draws us away from faith and the practice of modest compassion. The influence of evil is evident in video games that make deadly violence and sexual aggression entertainment. Power and domination are elevated as values. The media is progressively pouring that philosophy into the psyche of viewers. Addiction to this material is now commonplace among adults as well as youth. The trend is seriously affecting how people judge good and evil.

Raimond Gaita's *Good and Evil* is a dialectical argument that proposes there is evil in the world, not simply because people do things considered bad because of poor judgment, but that there are bad people who do bad things. Gaita makes an interesting point on the discernment of evil in respect to the Socratic paradox that if we know what evil is we would not do it. The related paradox of the day Gaita says is the claim that we can identify evil but rarely if ever do so in the behavior of others, which is frequently the case in respect to acquaintances. That needless to say is difficult because of the bond we have with friends and family. What that leads to is not simply as is often the case with an alcoholic spouse or with permissive parents of enabling but to the numbing of one's sensitivities to what is morally correct. [42] Gaita's argument applies well to the negative influence of acquaintances on our lives. The benefits of maintaining friendships or some perceived advantage in tolerating someone can anesthetize us to that fact. Candor is often confused with intolerance. But the very ability to identify evil can be an opportunity not only to counter the influence but also to do good for the person. That ability as Gaita says seems lost.

As to Socrates' presumed paradox people do gravely evil things and are quite aware of that fact. One would wish to think that if only we knew the truth we would follow it. The fact is that even if

---

[42]Gaita, Raimond. *Good and Evil. An Absolute Conception.* 2nd Edition. London: Routledge, 2004. p. 229.

men knew the truth they would unfortunately choose to reject it unless they were open to that gift of grace which not simply enables one to acknowledge truth but to also embrace it in their lives.

New Age thought has influenced all walks of life including members of the church. The 1989 censure of Fr. Matthew Fox OP by then Cardinal Josef Ratzinger concerned the former's New Christianity. Fox preached a paradigm shift, a radical change of belief to an impersonal Cosmic Christ present in nature. New Age is popular because, similar to Gnosticism, it is filled with mystery and excitement. It speaks of the divinity within and limitless possibility. The human intellect according to New Age psychology teaches the mind has within it all the capabilities of God. Faith is exercised by God as well as man, and man can exercise the same faith that enabled God to do great things. Therefore a person in touch with their divine nature can word dramatic and wonderful events.

The new theology, which refers to the transformation of traditional Christian doctrine to compatibility with New Age beliefs, teaches that God so loves us that there is little we can do to undo our relationship with him. Forgiveness and amending one's life is not an issue. We simply require faith in his goodness and in the fact that he already has given us a share of his divine nature. Gods of course can do no wrong insofar as they act with faith in themselves. New Age seeks the divinity within not God.

The crystals, enneagrams, astrology, charms, and ancient symbols are the paraphernalia of a widely divergent constituency of what is called the New Age Movement. What are more important are the essential New Age beliefs. The mind recreates existence because our consciousness becomes more than a phenomenological projection of things, but is empowered to change nature itself. What is psychically determined to be good becomes good. Good and bad, which replaces good and evil is absolute in line with the interests of the enlightened, divinely empowered consciousness. The appeal the movement has includes its adaptation to global concerns and values. Aidan Nichols notes that New Age rejects materialism, advocates meditation, and displays "enthusiasm for world peace."[43]

> The warmth of Mother Earth, whose divinity pervades the whole of creation, is held to bridge the gap between creation and the transcendent Father-God of Judaism and Christianity, and removes the prospect of being judged by such a Being.[44]

The association of nature with the divinity is ancient and has roots in Buddhism and Hinduism. Pantheism finds its home in views of existence that equate the natural with the supernatural and extraordinary psychic power with divinity. The New Age Cosmic Christ is present in nature as an impersonal divine force. But it is fully manifest in the minds of all the enlightened. Like Thomas of the Gnostic *Thomas Gospel* men and women who achieve a higher consciousness of reality are Christ. When they become one with nature they become gods. This is not the relationship of a man or woman renewed by a life of moral goodness in the image of the one Christ. Jesus of Nazareth has no more significance in New Age than any of the enlightened. Like the Jesus of Gnosticism he is "not your Master." Buddha has as much or more influence. As

---

[43] Aidan Nichols, OP. *The New Age Movement*, The Month. March, 1992. p. 88.
[44] *Jesus Christ the Bearer of the Water of Life. A Christian reflection of the "New Age." 2.3.1.* Vatican City: Pontifical Council for Culture, February 3, 2003.

such New Age thought has within it the dynamics of Antichrist religion. Adherents do not prefer the description of New Age as religion. Enlightenment and higher consciousness of truth is thought to transcend the conventional understanding of religious practice. Nevertheless the trappings of religion are apparent in rituals and mantra. [45]

Fr. Aidan Nichols advances two criteria that could effect such a dramatic change in society; one is the substitution of holiness with happiness, the other is grace with psychic power. The antichrist analogy is not hyperbole if we accept Sacred Scripture and the Fathers of the Church in interpreting New Age teachings. It is clear that this movement advances a malevolent self infatuation typical of the Satanic.

The misplaced priority of animal rights as equal to, and in cases of violence and death inflicted against loggers, fishermen, as superior to human rights and life is a manifestation of the pseudo-religious ideals associated with New Age thought. That this is misplaced value should seem evident to anyone when we consider the plight of so many humans. Why do we love animals more than persons? Is it that we presume like ethicist Peter Singer that animals are defenseless equals and deserve rights at least equal to human rights? Defense of God's creatures from inordinate treatment is laudable but the equation is not. As with Singer and others who champion presumed equal animal rights there is inevitable devaluing of human life in one respect or another. New Age has been examined here as a movement that is not completely integrated. It does not possess a doctrine that is universally accepted by those who claim to be adherents, and does not have leadership. Although considered a general trend it nonetheless can be identified with the beliefs, while acknowledging inconsistency

---

[45] Nichols, *The New Age.* p. 88.

and divergence, of its followers. That is not to say that New Age will not continue to define itself and that leadership will not be assumed down the road. The mistake however has been on the part of critics to throw out a net to sweep in anything that resembles a universal direction. The United Nations, for example, has been listed as a New Age organization. That aside New Age reflects a real movement that redefines Christ, and truth. We have already seen the resemblance of Gnosticism to New Age.

The discovery in Egypt of the *Gospel of Mary Magdalene* in 1896 and the discovery, also in Egypt, of the *Gospel of Thomas* in 1945, are the two apocryphal sources that are among the complex of causes that ushered in New Age. Mary Magdalene is depicted as a sage and favorite of Christ who evokes the jealousy of the Apostles. Like the Christ of *Jesus Christ Superstar* he has a sexual relationship with her. She teaches a new version of the resurrection, that the risen Christ is perceived as a vision of the mind, "which is between" the soul and the spirit.[46] This is a novel version of the human intellect or mind, the faculty of knowing. The mind here is distinct from the soul, the principle of life, and the human spirit, which is somehow distinct from both. It is contrary to the real unity of man, in which the mind is a faculty.

The implication in the *Gospel of Mary Magdalene* is that there is an entirely different realm of higher knowledge that is separate from the existential reality of the person. The resurrection is perceived by Gnostics, not as an historical event in time and place, which requires a real body, but as an arcane vision given within a dimension of knowing that is distinct from reality. As Paul says if there was no real resurrection from the dead then faith would be useless. The reason is sin. The real historical resurrection affirms that death, in the temporal and eternal sense, the penalty of sin, has

---

[46] Pagels. *Beyond Belief.* p. 104.

been overcome. Without a real flesh and blood resurrection sin and death prevail. The resurrection gives hope that living a life of virtue has more than temporal benefit. Some forms of Judaism, the conservative branch in particular, do not accept resurrection and afterlife. Their religious focus is on social and political justice. Some of our finest attorneys, legal scholars and other professionals come from this secularized Judaic tradition. My suggestion is that much more good could be achieved by Judaism if the freedom and worth of the person were assessed in view of man's immortality as the gift of divine love. While secularized compassion has merit divine love perfects.

Resurrection in this life, in its best sense, refers to a moral awakening, sometimes associated with recovery from the death of substance abuse and immorality. Another sense is the awakening to the self and unlimited freedom. This is the New Age perception of rebirth in the spirit. Within the Church the feminist movement is a manifestation of New Age emancipation and freedom in the spirit. Freedom in the spirit advocates a moral intuitionalism that is thought to transcend Church doctrine. It is basically Gnostic.

Liberty has become a byword for movements such as Dignity within the Church and society, which promote the normality of homosexuality in men. The tenor of these and other like organizations is toward the complete acceptance by our culture of homosexuality and lesbianism. Gay marriage is being defended in the courts as a right for that express purpose. The rationale is that similar to the previous ban on marriage between blacks and whites the refusal to permit gay marriage is an abrogation of civil rights. The equal protection clause of the 14th Amendment, which protects the civil rights of the person, was enacted after the Civil War to protect the rights of newly emancipated blacks from state laws. Consenting adults have the legal right to their sexual preferences.

But is there a constitutionally protected right for marriages that is not a contract between a man and a woman, and do we have the right to change the definition of marriage?

Freedom from the perspective of secularized culture is choice free from inhibition. One court justice defending abortion has said that "At the heart of liberty is the right to define one's own concept of existence, of meaning, of the universe, and of the mystery of human life."[47] Liberty here is devoid of any correspondence with reality and evades responsibility. The mistake is that if choice is not entirely personal it is not free. Choosing falsehood is not true freedom. The truth makes us free. As changes in moral opinion take place it is inevitable, unless there is a reinvigoration of spiritual values that bad laws will follow suite. That prospective change does not make the laws that redefine moral behavior correct. Aquinas' position that no civil law can justifiably oppose the natural law is more salient today because of this. If society continues to redefine itself by abandoning Christian mores then it will extinguish values that define humanity.

MARRIAGE

The Church urges understanding for those exceptional instances of "homosexuals who are seemingly definitively such because of some kind of innate instinct or a pathological constitution judged to be incurable."[48] This position from a Thomistic view rests on the supposition "that nature does not fail in all or in most cases but only in a few" (*Sent Ethic 1153b25-28.* Also as seen above

---

[47] See *Planned Parenthood of Southeastern PA V. Casey, 505 US 833 (1992).*

[48] *Persona Humana. Declaration on Certain Questions Concerning Sexual Ethics. VIII.* Sacred Congregation for the Doctrine of the Faith. December 29, 1975.

repeated in *ST Ia2ae 94, 4*). The ecclesial document *Persona Humana* is pastoral and advises that such persons who engage in a monogamous relationship be "judged with prudence."

> But no pastoral method can be employed which would give moral justification to these acts on the grounds that they would be consonant with the condition of such people. For according to the objective moral order, homosexual relations are acts which lack an essential and indispensable finality.[49]

Exceptions to nature do not replace the eternal law. The disorder whether elective or perhaps due to a rare accident of nature is the effect of original sin. All that afflicts mankind is the legacy of that sin. The sacrament of penance is obligatory for homosexual acts regardless of personal commitment. Judging with prudence does not preclude that.

Advancing gay marriage to a constitutionally protected right in effect attempts to convince society that homosexual relationships should not simply be tolerated as an expression of democracy but are natural and good. Sexual behavior is typically adapted and a nation's official approbation can further a pattern. Bad example can engender bad behavior. We are obliged to take this seriously for sake of the common good.

The spirit of the age encourages the exchange of reality with fantasy. Life for many has become an adaptation to virtual existence through the media. The transition from TV to computer screen to virtual existence with its broad spectrum of devices is deceptively easy. The amount of one's life spent before media is bound to be extensive. The eventual effect that this overload of technical stimuli and vicarious living must have is emptiness. Simulation simply does not satisfy the need to live life.

---

[49] *Persona Humana. VIII.*

Technology has created new worlds that stimulate the senses and alter the intellect's apprehension. The incessant chatter on cell phones often replaces needed human contact. Drugs increase sensual experience and relax inhibitions. What is real and what is not, what is good and what is evil become blurred. The film *The Matrix* plays on the confusion between the virtual and the real. That confusion has no basis in perception.[50] It parallel's the position of philosophers who repudiate the efficacy of sense perception. Confusion of the real with illusion is suggested by philosophers who claim to find no criteria to distinguish dreams from reality, from the mind and perception of the real physical world to nonsensical parallel worlds. This book stresses the importance of the apprehensive power of the intellect to make that distinction in sensible perception. The certitude of sensible apprehension is an essential factor in maintaining mental health. Self-induced doubt is delusional and anticipates schizophrenia.

There are ways to counter the substantial influence of technically advanced multi-media. We need to take time from them. The challenge is that many of us have little choice but to spend large segments of our day on the computer because of its integration with our work. Understandably it is a valuable and necessary technology for professionals. Nonetheless time can be better managed to recreate as well as engage in good works. If we subtract the remaining hours of the day there is time to interact with family, and occasionally visit friends, hospitals, assist the less fortunate, in general do works of charity. Often the loneliness we

---

[50] "If one is in a systematically deceiving world, how does one attain the ability to make reference to that world?" Carolyn Korsmeyer. *Seeing, Believing, Touching, Truth*, The Matrix and Philosophy. Ed. by William Irwin. Chicago: Open Court, 2002. p. 43.

experience evaporates with a patient's smile. Spiritual work has practical benefits for our self-esteem and sense of purpose. What we do with our lives and not mere words provides the best example.

Responsibility for what our youth consider okay rests largely with the convictions and example of adults and spiritual leaders. If that conviction is missing we cannot expect direction and example. Why do few parents and spiritual leaders speak out against the evil influence of much of our popular music and the amoral culture associated with it? There is a spirit of tacit defiance of Church teaching on faith and morals that is a mistaken perception of the inviolability of conscience. All have responsibility to form their conscience within the moral tradition of the Church. The witness of the saints and martyrs express that tradition most eloquently. These truths are the means of man's emancipation. Passionate love of God is seen in the martyrs who shed their blood for truths that in our unfortunate time are summarily dismissed.

New Age ideas, the enhancement of freedom, creativity, and happiness are attractive. Just as species evolve the human intellect is thought to reach new levels of understanding that transform itself. Rather than being the recipients of wisdom we become the source of wisdom. All the former prohibitions that limit free expression are expected to be transcended in the new epoch of Aquarius. Pisces, the presumed Christian era, is said to have reached its limits. The evolution of man is said to be entering a new stage that is radically different from its past. The Age of Aquarius foretells the expansion of consciousness and self-transcendence. Man enters into a new relationship with the divinity. No longer is the divine external to the self but is actually the realization of the true self. Man assumes the delusion of omnipotence.

The spirit of antichrist is in the world in various forms. Although there is benefit to be found in religious philosophies that teach inner peace through detachment—Buddhism being an example and forms of Hinduism being another they replace the fullness of truth found in Christian doctrine. Some of what Christ taught was adapted by Buddhism and Hinduism in cross cultural assimilation through the centuries. Buddhism today is not Buddhism of a millennium ago and neither are the many facets of Hinduism. We find terms like compassion that were not contained in their traditions being used in a way virtually identical to what we find in Christianity. Human nature is universal and men are in constant search of truth. That cannot be denied. So we find truths and half truths incorporated in religions and even political ideologies much of which has benefit to society at large. If however the fullness of truth is blurred within these various cultural movements they can be considered antithetical. That is the plight of man in the world. He is affected by many lights that are often presented under the guise of enlightenment but is really darkness that obscures the ascent to truth. Nonetheless there is despite obscurity the presence of light that uncovers truth.

WISDOM

Wisdom in its true form is present in the world. It is described in the biblical *Book of Wisdom* as ever present and moving as it wills. It is a gentle and pure light present in the order of creation. There it is cognitively present as the beauty and harmony of nature that reflects the divine law. Through it man may ascend by reason to acquire knowledge of the Divinity as First Principle of all that exists. He perceives good in what is good. He discerns order in creation as the basis of moral behavior.

Wisdom is also present to the mind in a special way through the Holy Spirit. Here truth is not acquired. Man is instead offered the gift of discerning moral principles necessary for salvation. A way to love is revealed to him that is a participation in the divine love. It surpasses his natural limits. He is offered the supreme gift of that knowledge of God given to those who seek to love Him.

The difficulty for man is in attaining wisdom because often staggered by cares and obsessed with pleasure wisdom is fleeting. He becomes jaded. Our intelligence often misses things it should know. We seek truth in places where it is not found. God in his wisdom foresaw man's difficulty in finding truth since his initial disobedience and fall from grace. Truth had to be made clear. It needed to become evident in that through which man knows best, the senses. Truth required personification in that which could be seen and touched. It required a voice. Truth had to come into the world of man as a man.

127

PART III
SUPREME TRUTH
1. JESUS

The greatest truth is identical with the greatest good. At the start I spoke of the correlation of being and good. All things created by God are good in themselves. God's wisdom can be perceived in them. All things possess their existence through the Divine will. They share in the goodness and beauty of their creator in accordance with their nature. Man unique among God's creatures reflects the image of God. That is seen primarily in man's intellect, which is able to apprehend things in accordance with their natures as well as being conscious of the distinction of his own being from all that he perceives. This innate capacity of reflexive comprehension is the entrée to man's knowledge of God. Man is able to penetrate beyond the physical and discern in creation goodness and order that speaks to a primary cause and First Principle of all things—distinct from his person and distinct from all that is visibly perceived. The initial knowledge of the world in sense perception then leads by reason to knowledge of the First Principle of all created things. Seeing the convertibility of being with good man discerns that the First Principle is God who is the source of good and as Supreme Being is perfect good. This train of thought is ancient and refers back to Plato and Aristotle. Aquinas improved it with his notion of First Principle of existence in *Essence and Existence.* Aquinas demonstrated that because the essences of created things are variable and limited they are not the cause of their existence. God, the First Principle of all things is unique in that he is not caused. As such what God is, his essence is identical with his existence. Man has the marvelous capacity to know that his notion of a transcendent God is not God. God exists beyond thought. The knowledge of Plato and Aristotle was limited by the human intellect. What distinguishes Aquinas is the revelation of Christ. In God alone being defines goodness. The Person of Christ does not simply manifest higher degrees of goodness but is the revelation of the Supreme Good.

> Something which has existed since the beginning, that we have heard, and we have seen with our own eyes; that we have watched and touched with our hands: the Word, who is life – this is our subject. That life was made visible to us. (*1 Jn 1, 1*).

Of all that is perceived and known in this life as true and as good the greatest of all is the knowledge of Christ. Since our salvation and eternal happiness depends on this knowledge God willed that the Divine Word be made manifest in visible flesh in time and place. Thus it was that Jesus of Nazareth was born in the world from the Immaculate Virgin that men might see, hear, and touch Him. That unique seeing hearing and touching could not be entirely limited to a time and place. Therefore the Apostles who possess the singular charisma of having been witnesses to the Resurrection handed on to us the account of Jesus' life in the Evangelical Gospels and in the teaching and correct interpretation of the Gospels contained in the Apostolic Tradition. That tradition is incorporated in a Church of living stones, members that both safeguard the integrity of the knowledge of Christ and His teaching and reveal Him to all men. The Church throughout history becomes the Mystical Body of Christ visible and tangible to the world in its members and in the sacraments, foremost of which is the Holy Eucharist. In the Holy Eucharist Jesus of Nazareth is present to us in the words of Paul VI in a most excellent way. He is present and visible to us in his divinity and in his humanity through the eyes of faith in the form of bread and wine. In fact in receiving the Holy Eucharist we receive Christ in a way that was not available to the Apostles until the Last Supper and the institution of the Holy Eucharist. In receiving the Holy Eucharist we receive His living fullness and our own eternal life.

Since the death and resurrection of Christ the Apostles ensured this propagation by ordaining ministers empowered by the Holy Spirit to live and preach the word of God. What exemplifies this message is the Word made flesh, someone like us in every way and with whom we can identify. Yet the Word made flesh is unlike us in that in Him there is not the darkness of evil. He is Light that in one sense as God is impenetrable but in another as man completely accessible and lovable. From the Cross he draws us to Himself. We are justified by the pouring out of His precious blood.

Now the fullness of man is exemplified in Christ. Jesus defines man and through Him we learn who we are in respect to our nature and what our direction and purpose is in this life. God made man in His own image and from all eternity sought to reveal the fullness of that image in Christ. While the Person who is Christ possesses the fullness of the divinity in his divine nature, the unique mystery is the union of his divine nature and his human nature. And it is in the human nature of Our Lord that we are able to discern the perfection of man. And through his humanity He reveals who God is. That discernment is not merely available to all but necessary for our salvation. Not all men admit to that discernment and may give reason for rejection. Now intellectual understanding and true intellectual assent as we have seen in examining conscience differ. The reason why the Cross stands to reveal what is in men's hearts is precisely because men do intellectually perceive the divine nature of Christ. That is because Christ, the Truth, reveals God's nature, which is Love. But many refuse to assent. Accepting Christ or not accepting Him as the Divine Word and Savior is the same as accepting goodness itself or rejecting goodness itself. While all persons are aware of good in their lives and similarly perceive good in Christ it is only in Christ that we perceive that perfect good found only in God. Accordingly all whether admitted or not perceive Christ as truth itself because truth and goodness is defined in Him. That is why to hear the gospel and reject it is to seal one's condemnation because to reject the Gospel is to reject the Divine Word who is Love. The written word of the Gospel is the Word made abundantly manifest to us. It exudes the holiness and goodness of God in the life and Person of Christ foremost so in His willingness to suffer and to die for our salvation. Furthermore as Augustine says Christ's most marvelous work is His Resurrection. Despite our condemnation of Him by our sins He does not condemn us but rises from the dead that we might live. To make sense out of the enigma of the Cross we have to understand what the divine love is, not in anthropomorphic terms but in accordance with revelation both in Sacred Scripture and as spiritually revealed. Saint John of the Cross said that love is repaid by love alone. Augustine believed that if any human act defines freedom it is to love, because authentic love is given as a gift. That gives rationale to Christ's holding back his power and his exclusive appearances after the crucifixion.

There are no arguments or evidence of the Word made flesh that precludes faith. The words Christ uses in witness to Himself, and the way of life He proposes have power to evince faith. Assent to truth is the pathway to eternal life. Now intellectual assent on one level is recognizing truth. But is not the commitment to that truth different from its recognition? Belief differs from faith. Perfect assent requires desire. This desire is motivated by spiritual love. It is an act of the will that assents to love, *which* is the basis of a living faith. Belief as a matter of course has its value. That was indicated above by Saint Paul in his letter referring to the pagan Romans. Saint Paul implies that if the Romans had followed their conscience and embraced what was clearly evident in the order of creation they would have elected to believe in God. Saint Paul's words suggest they would have been disposed to a higher level of natural law morality, and I would add perhaps the gift grace. Aristotle's great wisdom and grasp of moral truth is an example of those possibilities for the non Christian. While belief in God and the practice of a moral life is attainable through reason that practice remains insufficient without grace. The difference in respect to Christ is that belief is not simply based on visible evidence in the order of nature but by faith in the Person of Christ. The resurrected Christ and the Apostle Thomas shed light on this, "You believe because you can see me. Blessed are those who have not seen and yet believe" (*Jn* 20: 29). Sense perception of the resurrected Christ was evidence of His real resurrection and necessary for the Apostles to act as unimpeachable witnesses to that historical fact. And we are those who have not seen and yet believe. Christ says we are blessed in comparison to Saint Thomas who actually did see the risen Christ and touched His wounds. Christ wished to emphasize the value of belief based not so much on visible fact but on the disposition to love Him. Love is freely given to us and we respond with love in complete freedom.

If reason were the only means sufficient for salvation there would be no room for faith motivated to love. Reason can only take us so far. We reach a point when, as spectators, the truth of divinely inspired charity seems unreasonable. That is because this virtue cannot be the product of the natural light of reason. Faith is intellectual assent and more. It is the willful desire to believe and to do the will of God. Faith is a desire that exceeds man's natural ability. That is why the Apostle John says it is not that we have loved God, it is rather that He has loved us first. A living faith is purely a gift. The Apostles apprehended through the senses what was completed by grace, which is the desire to know and to follow Christ. The premise of the apostolic witness is that if we discern Christ we know the Father who is Truth. That truth is also the Way (*Jn 14*: *6*). The Way defines moral behavior. Christ is the way to life and truth. He is the cornerstone of the virtuous life. As the incarnate source of all good he is the exemplar of good.

The Cross of Christ is a contradiction. Paul on one occasion had decided not to preach on the Cross and experienced an embarrassing failure at the Areopogus (*Ac 17*, *23*). He had structured his lecture as an intellectual appeal for the audience of mostly philosophers who used the Areopogus in Athens as a forum for discussion. When he did speak of Christ's death and resurrection they laughed and left the auditorium. Shortly after he left Athens for Corinth and immediately preached the theme that would become his theological signature, Christ Crucified.

> The message of the cross is folly for those who are on the way to ruin, but for those who are on the road to salvation it is the power of God. As scripture says: *I am going to destroy the wisdom of the wise and bring to nothing the understanding of any who understand. Where are the philosophers*? *Where are the experts*? (*1 Cor 18-20*).

The contradiction of Cross is what draws us. There is no act of love that is greater than this. That Christ was crucified for our sins carries with it the effect that in sinning we condemned him. What should have justly resulted in our condemnation was transformed by his merciful goodness into our triumph over sin and death. It is a gift in the absolute sense. Through it Christ reveals that he is the supreme good. That is why the passion of the cross as the power of God confounds human logic. We cannot fathom its depth. It can only be revealed. Freedom is defined by our disposition to receive that truth. The truth revealed in Christ's passion indicates his passionate love for mankind. It sets us free. It yanks us out of our complacency and hurls us into the fire. Man is called to love God with passion.

Passion is part of man. But to genuinely love with the flame of passion requires intimate knowledge of the object of what we desire. The great challenge in this life is our knowledge of the divine nature. St. Anselm's prayer "Lord let me love you that I might know you and let me know you that I might love you" sums it up. Knowledge of Christ reveals the Father's identity. The depth of the love we find is fathomless. When we feel that we have found what we sought we realize there remains more to be revealed and are drawn further. We desire what is only known fully in the beatific vision.

The mystic John of the Cross speaks of that knowledge in poetic verse in *The Spiritual Canticle.* He seeks to convey divine love through poetry in the same manner that Solomon wrote about his love for a young woman in *The Song of Songs.* The Jewish people later rejected Solomon's work in the years following Christ's advent. The early Church selected it from among the many writings that were originally included in the Torah. The work was also later removed from the Bible by the Reformers but retained by the Catholic Church. The Church as did John of the Cross saw through its literal meaning and perceived its deeper spiritual sense of the love between God and man. The aesthetic sensual imagery and depiction of human passion is transformed into spiritual passion. It references the miraculous. Francis of Assisi is among those Aquinas alludes to who in this life are blessed with a more direct, intimate knowledge of God.

> Those to whom it is given to see God through His essence in this way are withdrawn completely from activity of the senses, so that the whole soul is concentrated on seeing the divine essence (*De Ver 10, Ad 11*).

Saint John of the Cross says this knowledge is still limited and not the fullness of the beatific vision. Prayer from the heart however does reveal something because otherwise we could not love God with passion. Augustine struggled with that asking how one could love what is not known. Now it is true that we can love an idea or a virtue like justice. However when we are charitable something inspires us to so love. That has to occur through the presence in us of something real. Theologians call grace the love of God. And that love can only be present in us if God is in us through the Holy Spirit. The person has interior knowledge of the presence of the Holy Spirit even if it is not quite the same as that experienced by mystics like John of the Cross or Francis of Assisi.

God speaks to us in quiet prayer. Often that interior knowledge is hidden. It is knowledge that the intellect cannot clearly understand and express adequately because it is not the usual way that we know. Its authenticity is in the witness the faithful give to Christ by works of charity, or even in charitable persons who do not oppose Christ.

Passionate love of God expressed in our love for the person of Christ is to love good. It is love of the supreme good that translates into our desire to be merciful and forgiving, and to selflessly pursue the good of others.

> There are four things involved in a virtuous act. First, that the substance of this act is modified in itself: This is why the act is called good, as bearing on fitting matter or clothed with fitting circumstances. Second, the act must relate fittingly to the subject, that is, be firmly rooted. Third, the act must be fittingly proportioned to something extrinsic to it as its end. These three all follow from the fact that the virtuous act is directed by reason, but a fourth is taken from directing reason, namely, deliberation (*Virt Card 1*).

An act that flows from within the heart of a just person changes the substance of the act. It becomes an act of divinely inspired charity. In it are encountered all the rational constituents of justice. It is consciously ordered to an extrinsic good that belongs to the other person. In other words it is literally an act of love. Aquinas perceived justice in those terms to describe this all-encompassing virtue. Justice carries with it the character of selflessness. We act in reasonable deference to the good of others. Charity perfects our love of others to the extent that our actions participate in the divine love.

There are examples of love that go beyond the confines of human reason. Mother Teresa of Calcutta's love for the dying poor of India, many of them untouchables, was a virtuous love that was passionate. That someone would volunteer to retrieve the dying outcaste, covered with filth, wash them, place them in a comfortable place, and show them genuine human affection—without ulterior motive such as conversion does not make sense from a rational perspective. Give them food and physical comfort but why touch them tenderly and kiss them? Teresa's wish was to demonstrate to them that they were not forgotten, that they were loved in a personal way for their own sake, and that if humanity forgot them God would not. That demonstration was an interior compulsion that required expression because of the divine love that filled her being. The expression of that love draws others. Many young high caste women joined Teresa in that expression of compassion for the least of their brothers and sisters. God chooses to express the beauty of his love through our humanness. That is because the very act of our existence was so that we might participate in the goodness of the creator.

Beauty in nature has historically been linked with the beauty of the divinity. Aquinas did not develop that theme. Beauty as reflective of the divinity is Plato's vision, and that development is left to the more Platonic philosophies of Saint Augustine and Saint Bonaventure.

Bonaventure was a contemporary of Aquinas and a Franciscan, who followed the pathway leading to knowledge of God, blazed by his religious exemplar Francis. For Bonaventure man perceives something of the nature of the divinity in the beauty found in creatures. The rational pathway is described in Bonaventure's doctrine of exemplar causality in his *Sententia* on Peter Lombard. Exemplar causality correlates with God's efficient causality and the purpose of final causality in the likeness of man with God. In the *Breviloquium*, called his most sublime compendium of dogma, all good is from God.

> Everyone exists by virtue of the efficient cause, is patterned after the exemplary cause, and ordained toward the final cause. For this reason, every creature is one, true, and good (*Breviloquium, II, 1. 4.*).

Exemplar cause for Bonaventure is similar to Jesus who is the Light in John's Gospel prologue. He is the spiritual light that dispels darkness. The light of God imbues his creation and its beauty reflects his. Bonaventure therefore perceived beauty in nature as the mirror of God's love and beauty. That beauty is preeminently evident in man when he participates in the divine love.

The tradition of contemplation in Catholicism from Augustine, Francis of Assisi, Bonaventure, and John of the Cross is rich with allusions to beauty and its exemplification in God. The doctrine's importance is that it presents us with an emotive path to knowledge of God. Here Aquinas agrees true love is emotive. Beauty is also an intellectual apprehension exclusive to man. It has power to draw. Bonaventure says that the apprehension of beauty in things draws us by desire to the creator.

Aquinas like his mystical contemporary Bonaventure relates the efficient causality of God to man's final causality (*Cm Meta 775*). Aquinas says if it were possible to attribute a cause to God in creating man, and that only hypothetically since God cannot be caused to act, that it would be His love for man. In that conditional sense love is understood as the cause of man's creation (*Cm Meta 782*). Man is created out of love to be drawn by divine love. Man's ultimate end therefore corresponds to his final end in Christ. Christ Crucified draws all men to himself. In this Christ is the end of man and exemplar of love that perfects our humanness.

Beauty is vividly perceived in spiritual love and emotive expression conveys the variations of empathy of the spirit. If God cannot weep for us, he conveys his sorrow in Christ. If he cannot suffer and die to demonstrate the depth of his love, he does so in the unfathomable mystery of Christ Crucified. The revelation of Christ conveys knowledge of the Father that otherwise is not possible to attain. Good is discerned at its highest level through Christ.

Passionate love is best understood in the passion of Christ. The disciple savors the good of a selfless and humble love given in freedom. The cross remains an absurdity and perplexing mystery for the world because of the unwillingness to experience its meaning. This kind of suffering for the good of others seems pointless. There are no visible rewards. Its power transcends the vision of the onlooker who is settled on self-gratification. To look upon Christ crucified is to be struck by a sword that literally reveals what is in our heart. To look without prejudice and preconceived contempt is to open the mind to a very different kind of power. It is this final step at which so many falter. Enter in and what is found is a peace and joy that cannot be found anywhere else. That truth is at the center of contemplation of God. We find in it Christ's love flowing from his Sacred Heart. It is a truth that reveals who God is. It is unique to Him and delightful to behold. Nothing else in this life surpasses the passionate desire to be like that which is known. In a mystery yet to be known and that the contemplatives have tasted in this world we become what we know. Nothing else will suffice.

The world cannot give to us what God alone can. Neither can anyone take it from us unless we give them that power. And that is to find in Him the truth. We perceive in Christ utter good. Faith and reason give us an understanding that there is only one source of happiness. It is not found in the vain love of self that proclaims itself. There is in that the nothingness and deprivation of good that typifies evil. Absence of evil does not reveal moral good. Christ alone is good and shows the way. Aquinas says that to the divinity of Christ we owe worship and to his humanity veneration. In the Person of Christ man renders that unreserved love deserving only of the Divinity. The other understanding of veneration is discerning the perfection of humanity (*ST 3a 25, 2*). He is exemplar, the way, the end, the truth, and life. That discernment and the desire to pursue this path of divinely revealed good distinguish our freedom and complete our humanness. Truth and the discernment of good are found in a being of immeasurable, personal love. To comprehend God's love then we must look to Christ Crucified. The Cross is Christ's marriage bed in which He consummates His marriage to His Bride, the Church. He invites us to find spiritual joy in the selflessness of the Cross. With it we participate in Divine love in the salvation of souls.

GRACE

Aquinas quotes Paul in *Rm 5, 1* stating that any movement toward God such as contrition is a meritorious act (*De Ver 28, 8*). Such an act however cannot be the cause of the infusion of grace. The infusion of grace precedes contrition: "Accordingly I say to you: Many sins have been forgiven her because she has loved much" (*Lk 7, 47*). The woman's love follows discernment of Christ's goodness. But that knowledge is itself a gift.

> To be moved toward God by free choice follows the infusion of grace in some sense by the order of nature, though not by that of time. Hence it does not follow from this, seeing that the infusion of grace is one of the requisites for justification, that the motion of free choice toward God follows justification. (*De Ver 28, 4*).

Free choice is explained by the gift of ingratiatory grace in man prior to contrition and justification. God, the efficient cause of movement first supplies by ingratiatory grace what makes a man pleasing to Him and worthy of salvation. This is the order of nature. Free choice follows. But man must be disposed to receiving grace. This healing grace is called operative. It becomes cooperative grace by the meritorious action of man's free will (*De Ver 27, 5 Ad 1*).

Man acts first on a human level in choosing God but in the order of nature receives ingratiatory grace and the disposition to consent and the willingness to act through the gifts of operative and cooperative grace.

> For if we view the order of nature in the line of material causality, the motion of free choice naturally precedes the infusion of grace as a material disposition precedes the form. If, on the other hand, we view them in the line of formal causality, the sequence is reversed. (*De Ver 28, 8*).

The woman who wept at Christ's feet depicted above in *Lk 7, 47* penetrated with the eyes of faith what the human intellect without grace cannot comprehend. Whatever God wills cannot be caused as if something in us were to cause Him to give us that grace. It is rather that God's will is productive of good in us (*De Ver 27, 1*).

God's love for us is so great that it causes that which makes us worthy of that love. God acts freely and not out of compulsion. Productive grace is purely a gift to those whom He chooses. God who is all powerful creates free will and nonetheless moves our will and we act in complete freedom.

2. IDENTITY OF JESUS

God is all powerful and all knowing. Time does not affect God's knowledge. He knows all things at once as a presence. God is pure act. There is no sequence of acts or knowledge in God. Because of this the creation is an act not measurable by time. Any measure of something must relate to something else by which it can be measured. There is no means of determining when the universe was created because there is no other preexisting physical coordinate by which to measure it. The real matter then is not when the universe was created but the fact that it was created. Yet within the universe all things are subject to time. The universe—though created by God and dependent on Him for its existence and who is its uncaused First Cause—is a distinct and separate reality that possesses its own laws of operation and autonomy in respect to events that occur within it. For examples Christ said God allows the sun to shine and the rain to fall on the good as well as the bad. He says that the death of those men crushed by the collapse of the tower of Siloam was not due to any sin that they committed as was thought by the disciples. It was chance. The exceptions to autonomy and chance occurrences are when God intervenes in the affairs of men. While there is no sequence of acts in God there is sequence of effect that occurs within creation. That is why the Word eternally begotten by the Father, was born into the world by the Blessed Virgin in measurable time. The Word existed eternally with God outside of time and therefore as the Apostle John says is God. Did the Word assume a body simply to manifest His divinity or was Christ a human person gifted by the spiritual presence of the Eternal Word? Nestorius Patriarch of Constantinople essentially taught the later, that Jesus of Nazareth was a human person with a special relationship with the Divine Word. Nestorius preached that the Divine Word was lord of Christ relegating Jesus to a human person [6th Anathema of Saint Cyril of Alexandria]. Nestorius denied communion of the Divine Presence by the flesh of Jesus taken from the Blessed Virgin [11th Anathema]. Thus Nestorius denied that the Virgin was Mother of God [1st Anathema]. The controversy was successfully addressed by Saint Cyril of Alexandria at the Council of Ephesus 431 AD. Saint Cyril explained the doctrine of two natures, one divine and one human, in the one Person of Jesus Christ. The Blessed Virgin was confirmed at that council as Theotokos, Mother of God.

Although Nestorius was condemned by the Council of Ephesus the controversy remained in the East until the Council of Chalcedon 451 AD when the doctrine of two natures was declared settled doctrine for the Universal Church. But the identity of Jesus remained an issue in the East. The Council of Constantinople 381 AD had inserted the filioque clause into the original Nicaean Creed. The clause teaches that the Holy Spirit proceeds from the Father and the Son whereas the 325 AD Council of Nicaea Creed cites only the Father. The difference is crucial to understanding who Jesus really is. The insertion of the clause was Rome's response to hierarchy of the Eastern Church who believed Jesus' two natures merged to the extent that He had only one will, a divine will. The West held that Jesus had a complete human nature. Ironically if we reduce Jesus' human nature to a cloak for the divine we return to Nestorius' position that the historical Jesus is not equal to the Word. As it pertains to his human nature Jesus is not equal to the Father. Insofar as the Person of Jesus is concerned He is equal. Jesus is one Person. That Person is divine. We cannot diminish the mystery of second Person of the Trinity since the fullness of truth and our salvation are exclusively in Jesus. We cannot construe "If you have seen me you have seen the

Father" to mean that Jesus is simply like the Father. He confirms his exclusive identity when says "Before Abraham I Am."

The title Theotokos given to Mary validates that the Word received His human nature from her and that to consume His flesh and blood is communion with God. The Blessed Virgin also has a special role in bestowing grace. Her Son is the One Mediator of grace. But when she gave her consent at the Annunciation she allowed for the flow of grace to all. She possesses a critical role. Saint Thomas Aquinas was unable to fully appreciate this since the doctrine of the Immaculate Conception had yet to be declared. He believed Mary like all mankind required her Son's redemptive act after her conception and that she was conceived with original sin. The Blessed Virgin does in fact play a significant role in Christ's redemptive act as the prefigured participant par excellence. God's unique favor in Mary's Immaculate Conception was part of His eternal plan for our redemption. He loved what He envisioned and knew—since God knows all as presence—and loves her far more than any other creature. Mary is the pinnacle of His creation. Jesus although born into the world by her is not a creature. Because the role of mother and son remains in heaven Mary is foremost as intercessor with her Son. We recall Christ's response to her authority regarding the water made into wine at Cana. That event has a lasting message. If one prays to Mary and she intervenes for us we can be assured that whatever grace she conveys to her Son on our behalf will be granted. Devotion to Mary is most beneficial for the reception of grace and for our redemption. Another consideration is that honor and love for our mother is divinely instituted. If Christ has so great a love for His mother does He not expect that we love her? Certainly He does. As shown John Paul II emulated Christ's love for His mother, which resulted in his greatness as priest, and world leader. To know Christ in depth we must possess a thoughtful and loving devotion to His Mother.

The advent of Jesus of Nazareth as pointed out is indispensable in revealing God's great love for man. Although God is pure act and essentially different from us we nevertheless are called to an exclusive relationship in this world that will be fully realized in the next. Then as the Apostle John says we will see Him as He is. That means there will be no intermediary between God and the soul in the beatific vision. The veil of the physical world will be lifted and we will possess the most intimate of all knowledge. Our spirit will enter into and be entered by God who is Spirit. While eternally united and becoming like Him we will still remain distinct and thus capable of the deepest personal love for Him. All that we find joyful and delightful in this life will be increased far beyond our present capacity to know in that great mystery.

The denial of a divine order in nature is the core error of those detrimental cultural movements that were examined in this text. While adherents accept the common sense knowledge of daily life they question the validity of natural law due to what was described as consequent ignorance. But if we assent to the irrefutable evidence of sense perception as the first principle of all knowledge we possess the solid basis of understanding human nature. We enter the pathway to wisdom and truth. Ultimately that quest for truth ascends to Christ. The Mystical Presence of Christ in the world is the Church, the preeminent source of truth. The Church combines faith and reason in addressing truth. The seeming anomaly however is that it is made up of sinners. Yet it is a body of sinners called to holiness. The entire body comprised of persons sometimes falling but never despairing, strive to follow a divinely instituted order. They give witness to the world of the presence of Christ. For those outside see the efforts of the many, the courageous faith of some, and the failures. They know something greater than its members is within assisting the fallen, inspiring remarkable compassion to the least fortunate, inexorably moving the whole body in the direction of truth.

Finally the mystery of Jesus' identity centers on his complete human nature. Thomas Merton describing contemplation in *The Ascent to Truth* correctly states that for man obedience to the will of God alone realizes spiritual union. Jesus the "Son of man" serves the Father in perfect obedience drawing the Father's great love for His Mystical Body. Jesus then is the Bridge to eternal life in God. Discovery of the supreme truth that is knowledge of Jesus Christ is similar to the analogy regarding scriptural enlightenment in *2 Pt 1:19* "Keep your eyes closely fixed on it as it were a lamp shining in a dark place, until the first streaks of dawn appear, and the morning star rises in your hearts." At times in a lonely place in the dark of night a light may shine within distinct yet intimately present. And it speaks to us of unspeakable goodness.

PRAYER

While we live in this world our most intimate contact with the divinity of Christ is in the Holy Eucharist. Insofar as awareness it is through prayer. Although this knowledge of God is imperfect and points to a more perfect knowledge in the beatific vision the sincere desire to know God and to love Him is met in a mysterious way by faith. While it is essential that we know who God is through the Person of Jesus Christ the interior knowledge we receive in contemplation is not through the senses, but through the darkness of a detached faith. The divinity enables those who seek Him with all their hearts, which is to relinquish all sensual desire to 'find Him.'

The evidence of genuine spiritual exchange with God is perceived in our actions. The apprehension of the ineffable goodness that is God inspires the man of prayer, prayer that is essentially dialogue and love of God to humility and meekness of heart. It is clearly understood that God alone is the source of all good and that the pursuit of our own will impedes his knowledge of His beauty and participation in His merciful love. If we do His will we manifest that beauty and mercy to others. It completes our humanness. Assent to this truth incorporates us with the Divinity. We become as it were likened to Christ, true God and true man.

Disdain for others, that utter contempt that signifies cruelty toward persons who are weak, who are perhaps sinful perhaps merely incompetent or for whatever reason is inspired by Satan. Merciful love, forgiveness, acts of kindness and prayer for them is inspired by God. We can be assured that whenever we ourselves are insulted, ignored, uncharitably avoided, falsely accused and chided, ridiculed, that is, held in vicious contempt—and we in turn respond with prayer and kindness toward our persecutors that God's grace is at work in us and that we are on the pathway to our salvation.

The hallmark of love is mercy. God loved us while we were still sinners as said by the Apostle John. He drew us to Himself not by any good act of ours but solely due to His merciful love. The proof of His infinite love and mercy for us is revealed in His death and resurrection. We condemned Him to death by our sins, since sin is itself a censure of good, which is God. He did not respond with condemning us but instead showed us great mercy. What then is mercy but love?

If anyone declares that he is without sin as the Apostle John says he makes God a liar. The key to true humility and the presence of the love of God within us is our acknowledgement of our sinfulness. Because God is infinite goodness there is much that we overlook in respect to our own unworthiness and sinfulness. An example is given by Our Lord to Saint Catherine of Siena in *The Dialogue.* He tells her that whenever we neglect to pray and offer sacrifice for our brother or sister whomever they may be that we ourselves are responsible for them by what He describes as our cruelty toward them. In other words to be insensitive to the spiritual needs of others and relinquish offering prayer and sacrifice for them is a denial of merciful love toward them.

The love of God in us is manifest by a passionate desire for the salvation of our brother and sister, for the weak and incompetent as well as for the proud and powerful. That love is never groveling but is courageous as well as merciful. The perfect exemplar for us to follow is Jesus Christ. The hallmark of Jesus of Nazareth's ministry then is not to condemn but to embrace all men as is finally demonstrated with arms outstretched from the Cross, "I will draw all men to myself." He draws all first by His infinite merciful love so that all may desire to abandon their former ways and to become like Him.

3. DEVIL IN THE SANCTUARY

Satan as Jesus said was a liar from the beginning. Satan's deceptive growing influence in the world is evident to anyone with moral perspicacity. The increase of opposition to the Church's authenticity, its relevance, the suppression of its freedoms, the continuous scandals affecting the clergy, hierarchy, the Vatican itself, and the increasing apostasy of the faithful, events perhaps simultaneous for the first time in history raise concern about end times and the Antichrist. What is offered on the subject by the media exceptions granted is sensational speculation motivated by financial gain and at times malevolence. Obsession with the occult is widespread. Many rather than exercise faith yearn for morbid entertainment and the spectacular. There have appeared, for a ready audience, misguided self proclaimed prophets who misquote scripture and seize on any writing no matter how obscure and bizarre that fits their oracles. For agnostics, the questioning academic, the uncommitted intellectual it is ground for rejection and greater contempt of religion. This brief account of the Antichrist is written to provide some form of reliable information for the reader.

The best witness to the truth about the Antichrist is what Christ has given the Church in his own words in the Gospels and what had been revealed by the Apostles in subsequent additions to the New Testament. Also included as reliable sources are the books of the Old Testament, in particular *The Book of Daniel.* I have written in the main text about the spirit of Antichrist. That is one manifestation of Satan in the modern world. The spirit of Antichrist has today and had been for millenniums manifest in the world. The anticipated manifestation of Satan in the last days of the world is who Christ and the Apostles Paul in *2 Thessalonians 2* and John in the *Book of the Apocalypse* speak of as a person.

When Christ left the Jerusalem Temple just prior to His Passion the disciples asked Him what was to become of the Jewish People's great center of worship (*Mt 24, 15*). Christ prophesied the Jerusalem Temple's total destruction and the great calamity to be suffered by the Jews in what is called the *Eschatological Discourse* contained in Matthew's Gospel. Following the 66 AD Jewish revolt the new but not yet universally proclaimed Emperor Vespasian in 69 AD still commanding Rome's 10th Legion [Nero prior to his suicide 68 AD appointed Vespasian to crush the rebellion] and his son Titus with another legion wreaked havoc on the Jewish homeland fulfilling Christ's prophecy. There are in this, Christ's lengthy *Eschatological Discourse* two prophesied apocalyptic contexts, one directly referring to 70 AD—"where the eagles gather there will be the corpse." This likely indicates the Roman legion standards and the death of the nation. The exact time of the other event is not given. It is during this latter event in which the appearance of the Antichrist is foretold. The reference in Matthew is not clear since the allusion is to Daniel's early prophecy *Dn 9:27* of the *abomination of desecration.* Daniel's prophesy was first realized in 168 BC when the ruling descendant of the Macedonian Seleucid dynasty established by Alexander the Great, Antiochus Epiphanes placed a statue of Zeus in the Jerusalem Temple. Antiochus Epiphanes means 'god manifest' and he likened himself to Zeus. He assailed the Jewish people killing many for refusing to believe in his personal deity. As such Antiochus Epiphanes was the first type of Antichrist and whose effigy of Zeus fits the description of abomination of desecration. Christ's allusion to the abomination of desecration seems to occur anew when Roman legions may have placed their standards and emblems within the Temple precincts and perhaps Vespasian having entered. The Roman cult of emperor gods was already in vogue. But the more significant suggestion by Christ is to the other future apocalyptic event of which the Apostle Paul says of the Antichrist that "*he enthrones himself* in *God's* sanctuary and claims that he is God" (*2 Th 2*, *4*). There is close similarity with Antiochus Epiphanes who was indeed a prototype of the more significant future Antichrist. Saint Paul places the appearance of the Antichrist immediately prior to the second coming of Christ. Christ's Second Advent will be revealed in His glorious appearance in the heavens. This precipitates Christ's final triumph over Satan and the Antichrist, and the Final Judgment.

The Apostle Paul speaks of a great revolt by members of the Church prior to the Antichrist's appearance. Apostasy or *apostasia* in Greek literally means renunciation, in this case belief in Christ not simply leaving the Church. John describes this apostasy in *Rv 13*, *12-14*. As regards the present situation of the Church and questionable events it is important to know that the Great Apostasy isolates an event that is readily recognizable and which will immediately precede the appearance of the Antichrist.

There are it seems in our present time discernible reasons for questioning and concern. Today's widespread abandonment of the faith fits the description of apostasy, though not perhaps Great Apostasy. Causes are increasing scandals, spreading of error, insipid preaching and bad example by us, the clergy. Most specifically devaluation of the Holy Eucharist and abandonment of the Sacrament of Reconciliation are the likely precursors of the prophesied Great Apostasy. Each affects the other. They are surely the catalyst of the present falling away. Refusal to acknowledge our sins and presumption desecrates Holy Communion and insults God by minimizing the love shown in the sacrificial offering of His Son. Unwillingness to acknowledge sin and refusing Holy Confession perforce degrades our estimatión of God's supreme goodness and the immense reality of God's infinite goodness present in the Eucharistic. If we do not actually believe in the Real Presence and refuse to recognize our sins what incentive will there be to regularly attend Sunday Mass or to follow Church teachings on faith and morals? Unfortunately in many parishes few of our youth attend Mass. The elderly hang on in spite of the current state of affairs and the tremendous pressure on the faithful from an increasingly secularized culture. Unless something dramatic takes place to reinvigorate clergy and inspire the faithful the trend will likely continue in the wrong direction to a recognizable Great Apostasy.

As to the identity of the Antichrist the Apostle John in the *Book of Revelation* makes reference to two Antichrist figures, the first *beast* that emerges from the sea and the second *beast*, who is his prophet that emerges from the earth. The first paves the way for the second and the second beast gives homage to the first. It is during the reign of the second beast, the false prophet that the Great Revolt, the apostasy of Christians and worship of the first beast and the Dragon reaches its climax (*Rv 13*, *14*). Christ in *Mt 24*, *24* alludes to these two Antichrist figures, "false prophets who will arise and produce great signs and portents" to deceive the faithful.

The Antichrist figure sets himself up in God's sanctuary and is the primary figure of Antichrist. He claims to be God and demands worship. But it is the first beast that appeared mortally wounded but then was 'miraculously' healed resembling Christ's resurrection (*Rv 13*, *12-13*), and who also demands worship. The first beast then resembles the Dragon and seems comparable to Satan, who as Lucifer sought to be worshipped like God. Lucifer means bearer of light or morning star, an indication of his original resplendence when created by God. Jewish tradition tells us that he became enamored of himself and sought to be worshiped in equivalence to God. There is in this self love the universal pattern of distancing oneself from and disobedience to God. Because of this Lucifer was cast into hell by Saint Michael the Archangel. The name Michael means 'Who is like God!'

The *Book of the Apocalypse* of the Apostle John is written in the prophetic style of similar writing in the OT, the prophecies and visions of Daniel. The use of imagery with apparently hidden meaning is widely implemented by John in this last book of the Bible. Hidden meaning seems to fit in with John's unwillingness to offer any compliance with the Emperor Domitian 81-96 AD who made unconscionable demands including being worshiped, and to deny Domitian access to the Book's true meaning, which clearly condemns the kind of false claim Domitian makes about his deity. The Apostle John at the time of the writing was already exiled to Patmos. So, can we try to glean actual meaning from John's more hidden texts? Certainly the author intended this last testament to be read and understood by the Church. Therefore, I will offer a reasonable if perhaps not entirely precise interpretation.

The "huge red dragon which had seven heads and ten horns" (*Rv 12, 3*) that threatens the woman about to give birth apparently a reference to The Blessed Mother is viewed as such in accordance with later interpretations but the earlier interpretations perceived the Woman as the Church. Jesuit scholar Jean-Louis D'Aragon in his commentary on the *Apocalypse* in the *Jerome Biblical Commentary* prefers the earlier view. That is an interpretive judgment call since it cannot be verified. And there is no viable reason to preclude that a prophetic reference to Mary cannot be coupled with reference to the Church. Mary was given the title of

Theotokos at Ephesus and Mother of the Church by Paul VI. The description in the *Book of the Apocalypse* of a woman clothed with the sun with the moon under her feet and crown of twelve stars on her head about to give birth to no other than Christ is so obvious a reference to Mary that to neglect a more serious consideration seems amiss. Exegetical science should account for what may be the mind of the Holy Spirit, not simply the mind of the prophet at the time and to not assess everything in a limited archeological, historical context. There is viability in the earlier interpretation but as said not to the exclusion to the latter. Furthermore, while the Apostle John was writing in the context of his historical time we can be assured that his writings inspired by the Holy Spirit also make prophetic reference to the actual second coming of Christ and the prior appearance of the Antichrist.

The Apostle John having been exiled to the island of Patmos likely made reference to Emperor Domitian when writing the *Apocalypse*. Domitian was a persecutor of the Church like his predecessor Nero, who was the first emperor to persecute Christians. Nero was consequently presumed by early commentators as the person who fits the description of the number 666 given by John to indicate the Antichrist. As Fr D'Aragon points out it also fits the view that Domitian was representative of the Roman Empire and representative of the Beast that recovered from his wound, Nero, who died, and was the original Beast from the sea. Domitian continued the persecution of Christians and resembles the Beast's recovery. What the Apostle John had in mind at that time needs also to be understood by the contemporary reader to have its more pertinent reference to actual end times and the Final Judgment of mankind by Jesus of Nazareth.

The description of the Dragon is similar in description to the first beast. The first beast that emerges from the sea also has seven heads and ten horns. Fr D'Aragon as do others views the seven heads as the Seven Hills of Rome and the horns as successive emperors. The difference is that the Huge Red Dragon's seven heads are crowned but not the horns while the first beast's ten horns have crowns not the heads. Fr D'Aragon does not refer to the distinction but does agree in the likelihood of transference of authority. The crowned heads of the Dragon indicate sovereign possession of authority and conference of authority to the first beast that emerges from the sea. The Dragon, by all indication Satan who first appeared as the Great Red Dragon in *Rv 12* is indeed said to confer his authority, and "his throne" on the first beast *Rv 13, 2-3.* The allusion here is to a messianic role. A question arises as to what form the first beast assumes at the end times, whether it be human or otherwise. The first beast is mortally wounded but 'miraculously' recovers in imitation of Christ's death and resurrection. Nevertheless the first beast may be the spirit of Antichrist in the world, or some ideological or religious entity preparing the way for an Antichrist person and the final revelation of Satan. At the time of its writing the reference is quite feasibly to the Roman Empire. Satan can appear in the form of a human person but cannot assume a real human nature. That power is reserved to the Divine Word. But Satan may deceptively assume the appearance of a person leading people to believe that the first beast is a man empowered by the Dragon. As the Apostle John says the multitudes will worship the Dragon for having empowered the first beast *Rv 13, 4.* Whatever the first beast may be in our time or actual end times insofar as to its form—it could well be a political ideology, a movement like secular humanism, perhaps a violent uncompromising religious sect—its recovery indicates its presence and power reappears in the world.

The second beast assumes the role as the first beast's prophet and is similarly empowered, presumably by the Dragon who empowered the first beast to dominate and rule the world. Neither the first or second beast then is the Dragon. Also noteworthy is the description of the second beast that emerges from the earth. We recall 'From earth you were formed and to earth you shall return' here an apparent reference to a human. He is described as a lamb with two small horns who sounds like a dragon (*Rv 13, 11*). He then is not the Dragon, but "a lamb" who imitates the Lamb of God. This second beast, the false prophet is clearly a type of messianic figure who has a statue of the first Beast placed in the temple to be worshipped. This statue comes alive, is able to speak, and demands complete subservience and worship under the penalty of death. The second beast appears to be a man, a human under control of the Dragon. As the Dragon's proxy the second beast 'sounds like the dragon' in proclaiming the words given him by the Dragon, mimicking Christ, who spoke the words of the Father. This resembles one who would claim to be the true messiah awaited by the Jewish people mainly orthodox Jews. There is also here the similar belief of Shiite Muslims about the apocalyptic return of the Second Imam. It is certainly reasonable to assume as do many of the Church Fathers that the Antichrist will repudiate Jesus of Nazareth literally fulfilling the meaning of antichrist. Repudiation need not be direct but may consist in refusal to assent to the Holy Spirit and Christ's teaching.

The first beast's description, the beast that emerges from the sea has authority and resembles the Dragon but is not the Dragon. The first beast we recall receives authority. It is Satan who desires worship whether directly or by proxy. Evil doctrine and behavior as seen can assume a form of proxy. The arch Antichrist is Satan himself who alone would assume to be god and demand worship, taking his place within the Temple in Jerusalem and seeking to exercise supreme authority. The second beast, the messianic false prophet is the Antichrist who will proclaim Satan and his doctrine of evil. As his prophet he occupies the Sanctuary in league with Satan. As Scripture says the Antichrist will place an effigy of the first beast, which like Antiochus Epiphanes' effigy of Zeus is the abomination of desecration. Saint Paul in *2 Th 2* speaks of the "Rebel" and "Son of perdition" as the one who occupies the temple sanctuary and proclaims that he is god. There is some ambiguity here. The "Rebel" would seem to indicate Satan while the "Son of Perdition" is already used in the Gospels in reference to Judas Iscariot. But it is not unfeasible that an evil human person another type of son of perdition in league with Satan may proclaim himself to be god as was the case with Antiochus Epiphanes. Eve assumed she would be a god by disobeying the Father. Such a person [the Antichrist] in any event must assume an identity with the evil that represents the first beast. The effigy placed in the Temple by the second beast, the Antichrist, represents satanic dominion.

Insofar as which Temple will be occupied by the Dragon some authors including Catholic believe it will be Saint Peter's Basilica. Although this account of the Antichrist is centered on Sacred Scripture I will comment on private revelation. In that regard there is mention of an antipope who will procure the role of Antichrist. Saint Hildegard of Bingen an 11th century German Benedictine prioress speaks of an anti-pope type of Antichrist who contests with the true Roman Pontiff and causes a schism. Saint Pius X according to sources foresaw a successor a fugitive from the Vatican. There are other similar prophesies attributed to saints all of which if authentic are nevertheless private revelation. As pointed out by Thomas Aquinas such prophesies may be from the heart of the prophet and not necessarily from God.

Anti-popes have existed. Although another antipope is possible it does not seem likely that the Antichrist will seat himself in the Chair of Saint Peter. That is because it suggests the falsehood that the gates of Hell will have prevailed against the Rock that is embodied in the Seat of Christ's Church. Christ assures us that the gates of hell will not prevail against the Church. While Saint Peter is designated the Rock by Jesus it is Jesus who is the true Rock that undergirds the Chair of Saint Peter and the Church. Furthermore the majority of Church Fathers are in agreement here. Their opinion is that the scriptural references are to the Temple in Jerusalem. Certainly that is what the Apostle Paul had in mind in *2 Th 2, 4* since Rome was not then the center of the Church. Jerusalem was. The arch Antichrist is Lucifer. He will repudiate Jesus Christ and it seems unlikely that he would occupy the very sanctuary, the Chair of Peter that represents Him Who he must repudiate.

Presently there is controversy particularly among extremist claimants to Roman Catholic orthodoxy that the retirement of Benedict XVI and the election of Francis I provide grounds for an anti-papacy. That controversy is unfounded insofar as Pope Francis is duly elected and Benedict XVI freely abdicated and does not claim to be Pope. There are comparisons made here of Saint Malachi's alleged prophecy [the prophecies attributed to Malachi—at least regarding Peter the Roman have been challenged as false] of papal lineage listing Peter the Roman as the last. Whether what is attributed to Malachi is reliable prophecy the presumed Peter the Roman is not likely to be the Antichrist nor will any other successor to the papacy. These comparisons at this stage of history are simply unfounded speculation. And the danger is that Catholics who presume to be orthodox but lack a balanced faith will assume that Pope Francis because of his innovative pastoral approach to issues is the Antichrist. The reliable sources regarding the Antichrist are more clearly seen in this context to be Sacred Scripture and not speculation.

It would seem the perfect Antichrist figure is one who claims to be the Messiah predicted by the Bible but is not. The Holy Land has been recovered by the Jews. The Temple site in Jerusalem is now under Israel's jurisdiction. The Jews believe that the true Messiah is yet to come. Satan has in that expectation a more historically and theologically developed environment for the Antichrist. There are proponents in Israel for reconstruction of the Temple. Now it is significant that the Jewish priesthood ended with Rome's destruction of the Temple circa 70 AD, since it was the only place where priestly sacrifice could be exercised under Jewish Law. The priesthood of the Roman Catholic Church took its place at that time and has since continued. Scripture alludes to a time when the sacrifice of the Mass will be abolished (*Dn 12:11*). That would likely occur during the reign of the Antichrist. That may coincide with a resumption of the Jewish rite of priesthood, perhaps in some new form. Although Islam's Dome of the Rock centered within the original Temple precincts poses an obstruction to plans for reconstruction we cannot predict what arraignments or events may transpire. Saint Paul believes the remnant of Jews will at the end of time turn to Christ. During the reign of Antichrist, who Saint Cyril of Jerusalem, Saint Irenaeus of Lyon and other Fathers of the Church say will at first deceive the world by the pretension of benevolence—the depravity and murderous disposition of Satan will eventually be revealed and the Jews will realize the error of their rejection of Christ. The full disclosure of Satan's malevolence will underscore the infinite goodness and merciful love of Jesus of Nazareth. Christ will not forget His promises to the Jewish people. In that regard it is noteworthy that

Saint Paul the Apostle always first approached and preached Christ to the local synagogue prior to preaching Christ to the gentile population of that area.

We do not know exactly how future events will unfold except Sacred Scripture's testament that the Antichrist will be a man, and that "the Rebel" will enthrone himself in God's sanctuary as if he were god. That prior to this there will be the 'Great Apostasy,' a falling away from the Catholic Church and Christianity in general and the repudiation of belief in Jesus of Nazareth. But repudiation may not be aimed directly at the Person of Jesus but remain in the form of the spirit of antichrist but which now contrived by the Antichrist effectively diminishes His doctrine. 'If you love me you will keep my commandments' (*Jn 14:15*). We already see a general mitigation of traditional doctrine on faith and morals which in effect is refutation of Jesus.

Nonetheless the time of Apocalypse may be distant and there may soon be a resurgence of faith in Christ. Patience and peaceful trust in the words of Christ characterize faith. We can never underestimate the effect of Christ's grace, prayers and sacrifices of the faithful and the power of the Holy Spirit. Prayer and a holy life is our present mission. Compassion toward all is the test of our faith in Christ. Hope and joy are the hallmark of a holy life. The adage love the sinner but hate the sin remains true. Whatever that sin may be we keep in mind our own sinfulness and that but for the grace of God we would be doing the same if not worse. Whatever age we may be in—the advancement of faith in Christ motivates us to significantly address the needs of the poor, to defend the weak, to be willing to suffer injury in imitation of Christ, to seek the good of the offender instead of retaliation, and to be constant in prayer and sacrifice for the conversion of sinners. We must be selfless that Christ may be evident in our life.

The direction of the Church toward truth and justice then is largely dependent on the holiness of the common faithful and its leadership. What is written here is a reasonable account based on Sacred Scripture and the views of Church Fathers about the end times and the Antichrist.

4. FINAL TRIUMPH

Christ will vanquish Satan when He returns to judge the world. Faith in Christ is the measure of our moral awareness and willingness to persevere in trying times. We live in a time of religious ambivalence. Example, social justice cannot be exclusively defined as sharing goods with the poor because it minimizes the fullness of Truth that is Christ. Surely Christ taught more than sharing goods. Ideologies like secularism, Marxist socialism, and so-called progressive thought within and outside the Church are antithetical to Christ. The witness of the many martyr saints who throughout history shed their blood for sake of evangelization, of chastity, for refusing deviate sexual advances as did the Uganda martyrs, for believing in the sanctity of marriage between one man and one woman, who protested infanticide, who firmly believed in and preached the necessity of confession of sins to a priest, and in the need to forgive sins, who believed and preached mortification of the body for sake of purity of motivation and respect of others, who practiced true justice in giving others their due, in respect of each person's human dignity, these many kinds of witness to the faith are the real measure of our faith in Christ.

The profession of faith we make every Sunday compels us to preach the Gospel in season and out of season. We have the serious responsibility, particularly clergy, to point out the errors of our brother. Saint Augustine makes the powerful analogy between the prophetic witness of the Old Testament to that truth and its correspondence to the priesthood of the New Testament. Nonetheless we are living in a world of increasing disparity between rich and poor. Poverty and inequality are largely the effect of unbridled capitalism. Capitalism places the accumulation of wealth as its ultimate goal. Free enterprise by definition differs. Anyone should have the right to engage in financial industry and the best of its kind is within a culture holding to Christian doctrine. That means fairness in respect to justice and willingly sharing with the less fortunate our wealth not by coercion as done in socialistic secular governed societies. Coercive government measures that appropriate funding from individuals and societal entities for sake of universal economic equanimity suffocate the spiritual life of the people inhibiting incentive for personal charity, and also for entrepreneurship. Notwithstanding the historical evidence of failure in Marxist societies the Christian leader has a moral obligation to address the disparity between rich and poor even making it a primary focus for practice of the faith. This should be encouraged by Christian leaders insofar as the teachings of Christ as elucidated within the Apostolic Tradition of the Church remain clearly confirmed and stated to the public. Government sponsored social programs can assist in narrowing the disparity between rich and poor and should be supported by Christians. Again the error is in the attempt to enforce universal economic equanimity. The very concept of economic equanimity in a free society is Marxist and tends to destroy freedom—since it empowers the state with exaggerated power whereas conscientious free assistance to the poor enlivens the individual and thereby the culture. Generosity and charity is the rule that defines true humanness, not enforced equanimity that dehumanizes individuals and culture. The Christian leader who firmly presents doctrine on faith and morals to the world, with discernment and compassion, presents the essence of the law which is love. Rather than faulting doctrine when he fails to succeed the honest pastor faults himself and seeks to improve. Laissez-faire behavior by clergy diminishes compassion toward the poor and those who struggle morally since compassion in a Christian culture of love requires divinely revealed definition. It is a beautiful thing when others know precisely what we stand for yet perceive in us the compassion and deep concern of Christ. The response is often remarkable.

Insofar as end times our own death is literally the end time. The mission of the faithful is to remain aware and to pray for the conversion of sinners. However events may transpire in the end Christ will prevail. The crucial issue for the individual however is whether He prevails in his own life. Christ speaks of losing one's life in order to find it. It is a reference to a spiritual death, a dying to this world with all its pleasures, awards, recognitions, consolations, gratification and the decision to live our life solely for Christ. Baptism is a spiritual form of death of the former and rebirth to a new life. The Apostle Paul says he is crucified to the world and the world to him. Saint John of the Cross refers to this death to sensual pleasure and entering into the darkness of faith. But it is a darkness in which faith reveals the Divine Light. It is through interior knowledge of the goodness of the divinity that we become aware of failings. But associated with this knowledge of God and personal failure is awareness of power He gives us to do great things, saving acts for our fellow man. Christ seeks to be enthroned within our hearts as Sovereign Majesty. This diminishing of self in order to allow Christ's goodness to be evident in our life does not diminish our person as uniquely individual with our specific talents and sentiments. Here the diminished self is surrender of a disordered will.

Acceptance of God's will, as our own is to express the beauty and goodness of God in all that we think, say, and do in our unique fashion. We need only to examine the extraordinary life of the Apostle Paul. All the saints are in fact different and their lives expressed their own creative dynamic. The freedom to realize that unique spark of life that is our person comes to full fruition only through the person of Christ.

The significance of Christ's human will and divine will is realized in the completion of our human nature and our salvation. Not my will but your will be done Father. Jesus gives us the example we must follow. His assent to the will of the Father is the assent of the Son of Man, the beloved Son of the Father who gives the Father in his human nature His complete assent. Redemption is made available to all humanity by Jesus' assent. Anthropology is complete only in our assent to the divine will, the will of goodness and mercy, of peace and compassion revealing to us the meaning of our existence and our eternal happiness.

165

INDEX

BIBLIOGRAPHY

Works by Saint Thomas Aquinas in Latin

Sententia Libri Ethicorum. Opera Omnia. Iussu Leonis XIII P.M. Edita. Tomus XLVII. Romae: Ad Sanctae Sabinae, 1969.

Ethicorum Aristotelis ad Nicomachum Expositio. P. Fr. Raymundi Spiazzi, O.P. Romae: Marietti, 1949.

SummaTheologiae. Blackfriars (English Dominicans). Thomas Gilby, O.P. Leonine and Piana Latin editions. London: Eyre & Spottiswoode, 1963.

Sententia Libri De Anima. Opera Omnia. Iussu Leonis XIII P.M. Edita. Tomus XLV, 1. Roma: Commissio Leonina, 1984.

Metaphysicorum Aristotelis Expositio. M. Cathala, O.P. R. Spiazzi, O.P. Romae: Marietti, 1950.

Physicorum Aristotelis Expositio. P. M. Maggiolo, O.P. Romae: Marietti, 1954.

De Ente et Essentia. Opuscula Philosophica. Raymundi M. Spiazzi. Romae: Marietti, 1954.

Quaestio Disputata De Veritate. P. Fr. Raymundi Spiazzi, O.P. Romae: Marietti, 1953.

Quaestio Disputata De Virtutibus Cardinalibus. P. Bazzi M. Calcaterra, T. S. Centi, E. Odetto, and P. M. Pession. Romae: Marietti, 1953.

Quaestio Disputata De Virtutibus in Communi. P. Bazzi, M. Calcaterra, T. S. Centi, E. Odetto, and P. M. Pession. Romae: Marietti, 1953.

Summa contra Gentiles. Romae: Apud Sedem Commissionis Leoninae, 1934.

De Demonstratione. P. Fr. Raymundi Spiazzi, O.P. Romae: Marietti, 1954.

Works by Saint Thomas Aquinas in English

A Commentary on Aristotle's De Anima. Translated from the Leonine edition by Robert Pasnau. New Haven: Yale University Press, 1999.

A Commentary on Aristotle's Metaphysics. Translated from the Marietti edition (Cathala-Spiazzi) by John P. Rowan. Chicago: Henry Regnery Press, 1961.

Commentary on the Nicomachean Ethics. Translated from the Marietti edition (Cathala-Spiazzi) by C.I. Litzinger. Chicago: Henry Regnery Company, 1964.

Disputed Questions on Virtue. Translated from the Leonine Edition by Ralph McInerny. South Bend, IN: St. Augustine's Press, 1999.

Truth. Vol. II. Translated from the Leonine edition by James V. McGlynn, S.J. Indianapolis: Hackett Publishing Company, 1994.

Summa Theologiae. Translated from the Leonine edition by Blackfriars. English Dominicans. London: Eyre and Spottiswoode Limited, 1963.

Selected Philosophical Writings. Translated by Timothy McDermott. Oxford: Oxford University Press, 1998.

On Law, Morality, and Politics. Edited by William Baumgarth. Indianapolis: Hackett Publishing Company, 1988.

Treatise on Law. (*Summa Theologica* Questions 90-97) Benziger Translation. Chicago: Henry Regnery company, 1965.

Works Referred to and Consulted

Aristotle. *The Basic Works.* Edited by Richard McKeon. New York: Random House, 1941.

Aristotle. *The Nicomachean Ethics.* Translated by H. Rackham. London: Harvard University Press, 1994.

Armstrong, R. A. *Primary and Secondary Precepts in Thomistic Natural Law Teaching.* The Hague: Martinus Nijhoff, 1966.

Ashley, Benedict M. OP, O'Rourke, Kevin D. OP. *Health Care Ethics: A Theological Analysis.* Washington, D.C.: Georgetown University Press, 1997.

Ashmore, Robert B. Jr. *Aquinas and Ethical Naturalism.* The New Scholasticism. 49 (1975) 76-86.

Berkman, John. *Medically Assisted Nutrition and Hydration in Medicine and Moral Theology*, The Thomist. 68 No. 1 January 2004. pp. 69-104.

Bonaventure, Saint. *Breviloquium II, 1.4.* St. Bonaventure. Volume IX. Editor Dominic Monti, O.F.M. St. Bonaventure, New York: Franciscan Publications, 2005.

Bourke, Vernon J. *Aquinas and Recent Theories of Right.* Proceedings of the American Catholic Philosophical Association. 48 (1974) 187-97.

Bourke, Vernon J. *Role of a Proposed Practical Intellectual Virtue of Wisdom, with Comment by Lottie H. Kendzierski.* Proceedings of the American Catholic Philososphical Association. 26 (1952) 160-178.

Bourke, Vernon J. *Is Thomas Aquinas a Natural Law Ethicist?* The Monist. 58 (1974) 52-66.

Bork, Robert H. *Slouching Towards Gomorrah.* New York: Harper Collins, 1996.

Bradley, Denis J. M.. *Reason and the Natural Law: Flannery's Reconstruction of Aquinas's Moral Theory*, The Thomist. 67 (2003). 119-131.

Brown, Raymond E. *The Birth of the Messiah.* London: Geoffrey Chapman, 1977.

Catherine of Siena. *The Dialogue of the Seraphic Virgin Catherine of Siena.* Edited by Algar Thorold. London: Kegan Paul, Trench, Trubner & Co., Ltd. 1907.

Cavanaugh, Thomas A. *Aquinas's Account of Double Effect.* The Thomist. 61 (1997) 107-121.

Childress, Marianne Miller. *The Prudential Judgment.* Proceedings of the American Catholic Philosophical Association. 22 (1947) 141-51.

Coffey, J. Patrick. *Personal Moral Reasoning and Impersonal Practical Wisdom.* Proceedings of the American Catholic Philosophical Association. 40 (1966) 145-51.

Curran, Charles E. *The Principle of Double Effect: Some Historical and Contemporary Observations.* Atti Congresso Internazionale. D/5. April, 1974.

Darcy, Eric. *Human Acts.* Oxford: Clarendon Press, 1963.

Davenport, John J. *Happy Endings and Religious Hope*, The Lord of the Rings and Philosophy. Edited by Gregory Bassham and Eric Bronson. Chicago: Open Court, 2003. pp. 204-218.

Davison, Scott A. *Tolkien and the Nature of Evil*, The Lord of the Rings and Philosophy. Edited by Gregory Bassham and Eric Bronson. Chicago: Open Court, 2003. pp. 99-109.

Deeken, Alfons S.J. *Process and Permanence in Ethics. Max Scheler's Moral Philosophy.* New York, N.Y.: Paulist Press, 1974.

Discher, Mark R. *Does Finnis Get Natural Rights for Everyone?* The New Blackfriars. English Dominicans. Vol. 80. No. 935. (1999) 19-31.

Ekbery, George E. *First Principles of Understanding: An Introductory Essay.* Oxford: Oxford University Press, 1949.

Elders, Leo J. *St. Thomas Aquinas' Commentary on the Nicomachean Ethics.* Studi Tomistici. 25 (1984) 9-49.

Eschmann, I. *St. Thomas' Approach to Moral Philosophy.* Proceedings of the American Catholic Philosophical Association. 31 (1957) 25-36.

Esser, Gerard. *Intuition in Thomistic Moral Philosophy, with Comment by Rose Emanuella.* Proceedings of the American Catholic Philosophical Association. 31 (1957) 156-78.

Fabro, Cornelio. *God in Exile: Modern Atheism.* Translated by Arthur Gibson. Westminster, MD: The Newman Press, 1968.

Finnis, John M. *Natural Inclinations and Natural Rights: Deriving <ought> from <is> according to Thomas Aquinas.* Studi Tomistici. Vol. 30. Lex et Libertas. Pontificia Acadamia di S. Tommaso. Libreria Editrice Vaticana. 1986. 43-55.

Finnis, John M. *Natural Law and the Ethics of Discourse.* The American Journal of Jurisprudence. 43 (1998).

Finnis, John. Grisez, Germain. Boyle, Joseph. *"Direct" and "Indirect": A Reply to Critics of Our Action Theory*, The Thomist. 65 (2001). 1-44.

Friedlander, Henry. Press, 2001. *The Origins of Nazi Genocide: From Euthanasia to the Final Solution.* Chapel Hill: The University of North Carolina Press, 1999.

Freud, Sigmund. *Analysis Terminable and Interminable.* (*1937*), *vol. 23.* The Standard Edition of the Complete Works of Sigmund Freud. Edited and translated by James Strachey. London: Hogarth Press, 1968. pp. 209-254.

Fuchs, Josef S.J. *Natural Law.* Translated by M. H. Gill and Son Ltd. New York: Sheed and Ward, 1965.

Gaita, Raimond. *Good and Evil. An Absolute Conception.* 2nd Edition. London: Routledge, 2004.

Galli, Alberto. *Morale delle Legge e Morale della Spontaneita Secondo S. Tommaso.* Studi Tomistici Saggi. Vol. 3. 108-151.

Garrigou-Lagrange, Reginald. *De valore reali primi principii rationis practicae secundum S. Thomam.* Thomistica Morum (Symp) 70-82.

Geach, Peter. *Mental Acts*: *Their Content and Their Objects.* London: Routledge & Kegan Paul, 1957.

Gilson, Etienne. *The Christian Philosophy of St. Thomas Aquinas.* Translated by L. K. Shook, C.S.B. New York: Random House, 1966.

Goebel, Julius Jr. *King's Law and Local Custom in Seventeenth-Century New England*, American Law and the Constitutional

Order. Edited by Lawrence Friedman. Cambridge, MA: Harvard University Press, 1988.

González, Ana Marta. *Depositum Gladius Non Debet Restitui Furioso: Precepts, Synderesis, and Virtues in St. Thomas Aquinas.* The Thomist. 63 (1999) 217-240.

Gula, Richard M. SS. *Moral Discernment.* Mahwah, NJ: Paulist Press, 1997.

Griese, Msgr. Orville N. *Conserving Human Life.* Braintree, MA: The Pope John XXIII Medical-Moral Research and Educational Center, 1989.

Griese, Msgr. Orville N. *Catholic Identity in Health Care.* Braintree, MA: The Pope John Center, 1987.

Grisez, Germain. *The First Principle of Practical Reason: A Commentary on the Summa Theologiae. 1-2 Question 94, Article 2.* Natural Law Forum. 10 (1965) 168-201.

Grisez, Germain. *The Way of the Lord Jesus. Vol. I. Christian Moral Principles.* Chicago: Christian Herald Press, 1983.

Grossman, William I. *Freud and Female Sexuality.* Journal of Psycho-Analysis. (57) 1976. 301-305.

Hawkins, D. J. B. *Nature as the Ethical Norm.* London: Blackfriars, 1951.

Hedwig, Klaus. *Circa Particularia.* Studi Tomistici: The Ethics of St. Thomas. Vol. 25 161-187.

Hicks, R. D. *Aristotle, De Anima.* Cambridge: University Press, 1907.

Hume, David. *An Inquiry Concerning Human Understanding.* Edited by Charles W. Hendel. New York: Macmillan Publishing Company, 1989.

Hume, David. *An Inquiry Concerning the Principles of Morals.* Edited by Charles W. Hendel. New York: Macmillan Publishing Company, 1987.

Jaffa, Harry V. *Thomism and Aristotelianism.* Chicago: The University of Chicago Press, 1952.

Jerome Biblical Commentary. Edited by Raymond E. Brown, S.S., Joseph A. Fitzmeyer, S.J., Roland E. Murphy, O. Carm. London: Geoffrey Chapman, 1970.

Jerusalem Bible. General Editor Alexander Jones. New York: Doubleday & Company, 1966.

Kaczor, Christopher. *Exceptionless Norms in Aristotle?: Thomas Aquinas and Twentieth-Century Interpreters of the Nicomachean Ethics.* The Thomist. 61 (1997) 33-62.

Kant, Immanuel. *Critique of Pure Reason.* Translated by F. Max Müller. New York: Doubleday & Company, 1966.

Kant, Immanuel. *Grounding for the Metaphysics of Morals. Kant's Ethical Philosophy.* Translation by James W. Ellington. Indianapolis: Hackett Publishing Company, 1983.

Katz, Eric. *The Rings of Tolkien and Plato: Lessons in Power, Choice, and Morality,* The Lord of the Rings and Philsophy. Edited by Gregory Bassham and Eric Bronson. Chicago: Open Court, 2003. pp. 5-20.

Kendzierski, Lottie. *Object and Intention in the Moral Act.* Proceedings of the American Catholic Philosophical Association. 24 (1950) 102-110.

Klubertanz, George P. *The Empiricism of Thomistic Ethics.* Proceedings of the American Catholic Philosophical Association. 31 (1957) 1-24.

Köhler, Wolfgang. *Address of the President to the sixty-seventh Annual Convention of the American Psychological Association.* Cincinnati, Ohio, September 6, 1959. American Psychologist. 14 No. 12 (1959) 741-764.

Korsmeyer, Carolyn. *Seeing, Believing, Touching, Truth,* The Matrix and Philosophy. Edited by William Irwin. Chicago: Open Court, 2002. pp. 41-52.

Kraus, Joe. *Tolkien, Modernism, and the Importance of Tradition,* The Lord of the Rings and Philosophy. Edited by Gregory Bassham and Eric Bronson. Chicago: Open Court, 2003. pp. 1371-149.

Kurtz, Paul. Wilson, Edwin H. *Humanist Manifesto II.* Amherst, New York: Council for Secular Humanism, 1973.

Kurtz, Paul. *A Secular Humanist Declaration.* Amherst, New York: Council for Secular Humanism, 1980.

Lévi-Strauss, Claude. *The Scope of Anthropology.* London: Jonathan Cape, 1969.

Lindon, Luke J. *The Significance of the Term Virtus Naturalis in the Moral Philosophy of St. Thomas Aquinas, with Comment by Richard J. Westley.* Proceedings of the American Catholic Philosophical Association. 31 (1957) 97-105.

Lonergan, Bernard J. F. S.J. *Insight.* San Francisco: Harper & Row, Publishers, 1978.

Long, Steven A.. *A Brief Description Regarding the Nature of the Object of the Moral Act According to St. Thomas Aquinas*, The Thomist. 67 (2003) 45-71.

Lucks, Henry. *Saint Thomas and Moral Sense*. Proceedings of the American Catholic Philosophical Association. 18 (1942) 117-20.

MacIntyre, Alasdair. *After Virtue.* Second Edition. London: Duckworth, 1987.

MacIntyre, Alasdair. *How Can We Learn What Veritatis Splendor Has to Teach*? The Thomist. 58 (1994) 171-195.

Marenbon, John. *Later Medieval Philosophy.* London: Routledge & Kegan Paul, 1987. Maritain, Jacques. *The Degrees of Knowledge.* Translated by Gerald B. Phelan. New York: Charles Scribner's Sons, 1954.

May, William E. *Aquinas and Janssens on the Moral Meaning of Human Acts.* The Thomist. 48 (1984) 566-606.

McInerny, Ralph M. *Aquinas on Human Action.* Washington, DC: The Catholic University of America Press, 1992.

McInerny, Ralph M. *Ethica Thomistica.* Washington, DC: The Catholic University of America Press, 1982.

McInerny, Ralph M. *Naturalism and Thomistic Ethics.* The Thomist. 40 (1976) 222-242.

Merton, Thomas. *The Ascent to Truth.* New York: A Harvest Book, 1981.

Messmer, Johannes. *Ethics and Facts.* St. Louis: B. Herder, 1952.

National Conference of Catholic Bishops [U.S.A.]. *Ethical and Religious Directives for Catholic Health Care Services,* Vol. 24: No. 27. December 15, 1994.

Nichols, Aidan OP. *The New Age Movement*, The Month. March, 1992. p. 88.

Nussbaum, Martha C. *Rules for the World Stage.* Newsday. April 20, 2003.

Nussbaum, Martha C. *The Therapy of Desire. Theory and Practice in Hellenistic Ethics.* Princeton, New Jersey: Princeton University Press, 1994.

Oates, Whitney J. *Aristotle and the Problem of Value*. Princeton, NJ: Princeton University Press, 1963.

O'Connor, D. J. *Aquinas and Natural Law.* New Studies in Ethics. Edited by W. D. Hudson.
Great Britain: The Chaucer Press, 1967.

Oesterle, John A. *Ethics: The Introduction to Moral Science*. Englewood Cliffs, NJ: Prentice-Hall, 1957.

Oesterle, John A. *Logic: The Art of Defining and Reasoning.* Englewood Cliffs, NJ: Prentice Hall, 1963.

Pagels, Elaine. *Beyond Belief. The Secret Gospel of Thomas.* New York: Random House, 2003.

Pagels, Elaine. *The Gnostic Gospels.* New York: Random House, 1979.

Pegis, Anton C. *St. Thomas and the Nicomachean Ethics: Some Reflectionson Summa Contra Gentiles III, 44, 5.* Medieval Studies. 25 (1963) 1-25.

Piaget, Jean. *The Child's Conception of the World.* Translated by Joan and Andrew Tomlinson. London: Routledge and Kegan, Paul, 1967.

Pinckaers, Servais, O.P. *The Sources of Christian Ethics.* Translated. by Sr. Mary Thomas Noble, O.P. Washington, D.C.: The Catholic University of America Press, 1995.

Pius XII, *Address to International Congress of Anesthesiologists.* November 24, 1957.

Pizzorni, Reginaldo M. *Il contenuto del diritto naturale secondo S. Tommaso d'Aquino.* Studi Tomistici. (Symp) 4. 191-221.

Pollan, Michael. *The Unnatural Idea of Animal Rights,* The New York Times Magazine. November 10, 2002. Section 6.

Pontifical Council for Culture, *Jesus Christ the Bearer of the Water of Life. A Christian reflection of the "New Age." 2.3.1.* Vatican City: February 3, 2003.

Pope Benedict XVI. *Jesus of Nazareth.* Translated by Adrian J. Walker. New York: Random House, 2010.

Pope John Paul II. *Ad Tuendam Fidem.* Boston: Pauline Books & Media, 1998.

Pope John Paul II. *Fides et Ratio.* Boston: Pauline Books & Media, 1998.

Pope John Paul II. *Veritatis Splendor.* Boston: Pauline Books & Media, 1994.

Rackham, H. *Aristotle. Nicomachean Ethics.* Translated by H. Rackham. London: Harvard University Press, 1994.

Reiner, Hans. *An Introduction to the Philosophy of the Existential Moral Act.* The New Scholasticism. 28 (1954) 145-169.

Rhonheimer, Martin. *Intentional Acts and the Meaning of Object. A Reply to Richard McCormick.* The Thomist. 59 (1995) 279-311.

Rhonheimer, Martin. *Intrinsically Evil Acts and the Moral Viewpoint: Clarifying a Central Teaching of Veritatis Splendor.* The Thomist. 58 (1994) 1-39.

Rhonheimer, Martin. *The Cognitive Structure of the Natural Law and the Truth of Subjectivity,* The Thomist. 67 (2003) 1-44.

Rommen, Heinrich. *The Natural Law.* Translated by T. R. Hanley. St. Louis: B. Herder, 1948.

Sacred Congregation for the Doctrine of the Faith. *Declaration on Euthanasia.* Sec. IV. 1980.

Scheiber, Harry N. *Doctrinal Legacies and Institutional Inovations,* American Law and the Constitutional Order. Edited by Lawrence Friedman. Cambridge, MA: Harvard University Press, 1988.

Scheler, Max. *On the Eternal in Man.* Translated by Bernard Noble. New York: Harper and Brothers Publishers, 1960.

Shanks, Hershel. *The Meaning and Mystery of the Dead Sea Scrolls.* New York: Random House, 1998.

Shirer, William L. *The Rise and Fall of the Third Reich.* New York: MJF Books, 1959.

Singer, Peter. *Practical Ethics.* 2nd Edition. Cambridge: University Press, 1993.

Skoble, Aeon J. *Virtue and Vice in the Lord of the Rings*, The Lord of the Rings and Philosophy. Chicago: Open Court, 2003. pp. 110-120.

Stern, Karl. *The Flight from Woman.* St. Paul: Paragon House, 1985.

Stein, Edith. *On the Problem of Empathy*: *The Collected Works of Edith Stein.* Volume 3. Third Revised Edition. Translated by Waltraut Stein, Ph.D. Washington, DC: ICS Publications, 1989.

Neuner, Josef S.J. and Roos, Heinrich S.J. *The Teaching of the Catholic Church.* Edited by Karl Rahner, S.J. Translated by Geoffrey Stevens. New York: Pauline Press, 1975.

Thérèse of Lisieux. *Saint Thérèse of Lisieux. An Autobiography.* Translated by Rev. Thomas N. Taylor. New York.: P. J. Kenedy and Sons, 1926.

Tolkien, J.R.R. *The Lord of the Rings. Part III The Return of the King.* London: Unwin Paperbacks, 1979.

Torrell, Jean-Pierre, O.P. *Saint Thomas Aquinas. The Person and His Work.* Translated by Robert Royal. Washington, D.C.: The Catholic University of America Press, 1996.

United States Court of Appeals for the Ninth Circuit. *Compassion in Dying, a Washington nonprofit corporation; Jane Roe, John Doe; James Poe; Harold Glucksberg, M.D., Plaintiffs-Appellees, v. State of Washington; Christine Gregoire, Attorney General of Washington, Defendants- Appellants.* No. 94-35534. August 25, 1997, Filed.

United States Supreme Court. *Dennis C. Vacco, Attorney General for New York, et al., Petitioners v. Timothy E. Quill, M.D., et al.* No. 95-1858. June 26, 1997, Decided. Prior History: On Writ of Certiorari to The Unites States Court of Appeals for the Second Circuit, Reported at: *1996 U.S. App. Lexis 26792.*

Verhaughe, Paul. *The Riddle of Castration Anxiety: Lacan Beyond Freud*, in The Letter. Lacanian Perspectives on Psychoanalysis, 6. Spring 1996. pp. 45-54.

Walgrave, J. H. *The Personal Aspects of St. Thomas Ethics.* Studi Tomistici. 25 (1984).

Wallace, William. *Existential Ethics: A Thomistic Appraisal.* The Thomist. 27 (1963) 493-515.

Wallace, William. *The Role of Demonstration in Moral Theology. A Study of Methodology in St. Thomas Aquinas.* Washington, D.C.: The Thomist Press, 1962.

Walsh, James. *Aristotle's Conception of Moral Weakness.* New York: Columbia University Press, 1963.

Weisheipl, James A. OP. *Friar Thomas D'Aquino.* Washington, DC: The Catholic University of America Press, 1983.

Wilhelmsson, John C. *The Transposition of Edith Stein.* San Jose, CA: Chaos to Order Publishing, 2012.

Westberg, Daniel. *Right Practical Reason.* Oxford: Clarendon Press, 1994.

Wippel, John F. *Metaphysical Themes in St. Thomas Aquinas. Vol. 10.* Washington, D.C.: The Catholic University of America Press, 1984.

Wittgenstein, Ludwig. *Lectures and Conversations. Lectures on Religious Belief.* Edited by Cyril Barrett. Berkeley: University of California Press, 1967.

Wittgenstein, Ludwig. *Philosophical Investigations.* Translated by G. E. M. Anscombe. Oxford: Basil Blackwell, 1968.

Wojtyla, Karol. *The Acting Person.* Analecta Husserliana. 10 (1969). Ed. Anna Teresa Tymieniecka. Translated by Andrzej Potocki. Boston: D. Reidel Publishing, 1979.

Made in the USA
Middletown, DE
24 June 2018